# Reserve Fund Essentials

**Jonathan H. Juffs**
**Graham D. Oliver**

**Oliver Interactive, Inc**
**Toronto, Ontario**
**Canada**

Second Edition
February 2008
(Fourth Printing)

---

**Canadian Cataloguing in Publication Data**

Oliver, Graham D.
Juffs, Jonathan H.
Reserve Fund Essentials

ISBN 0-9781986-0-3

---

# Reserve Fund Essentials

# Table of Contents

# PREFACE

This, we are proud to announce, is the Third Edition of "Reserve Fund Essentials", and our fifth printing. This edition includes several brand new chapters, including three on Operating Budgets. That's not to say that reserve funds are beginning to be short-changed — there's plenty of new material on reserves in this editions — but we had "things to say" about operating budgets, hence their inclusion.

First, why did we create RFE in the first place? Well, they say that inside every budding writer there are stories waiting to get out. And it was that way with us. We had a whole range of ideas related to reserve funds that we believed were worth sharing, but we had never really articulated them or organized them. This book has given us that opportunity.

Of course we also believe that our opinions, and the approaches we have come to favor, will be helpful to the vast numbers of people involved in the ownership, direction, and management of co-owned properties. That would include elected members of Boards of Directors, Community and Property Managers, Reserve Planners (also referred to as Specialists, or Engineers), Accountants and perhaps Lawyers specializing in this market. And let's not forget the hundreds of thousands (millions, maybe) of co-owners who, with great faith and expectations, write checks every month to keep their properties afloat and to enjoy their lifestyle.

There's a lot to learn about reserve funds and operating budgets.. We are not going to claim we've captured it all by any means. Which means that Edition Three will almost certainly be followed by subsequent editions as new ideas emerge. We're sure to receive more messages suggesting we add a chapter on this, or a few paragraphs on that. We very much appreciate feedback from our reading audience, and we hope it continues. Tell us what you would like to see in our future editions and comment, frankly, on material in this book you thought was not clear, or could "use some work" next time.

We hope you like our style. We have tried to make it readable (conversational, actually), and we've attempted to filter out ambiguity or obfuscation. We have not been shy about stating opinions throughout the book, and we know that our opinions will not necessarily be yours. Let's hear from you on those issues as well, please.

A final observation. That is ... we believe the interest level in reserve fund creation and management is lower than it ought to be. (Not so with operating budgets though). Seems to us that engaging a Planner to do a study, accepting the study (very often holus-bolus) and referring to it as seldom as possible is not a pretty picture. Particularly when your unit-owners' hard-earned money is involved. To the extent this may be due to a less-than-desirable level of understanding of reserves, we hope "Reserve Fund Essentials" will help, even a little, to improve everyone's comprehension of the vital place that reserves occupy in community living.

**Jonathan H. Juffs**
**Graham D. Oliver**

# Meet The Authors

First, we want you to know that we're very happy with the flattering remarks about our earlier editions that readers have taken the time to make. We don't mind admitting that a lot of hours have been devoted to all the aspects of putting together Reserve Fund Essentials, so hearing about its perceived merit makes us feel good, of course.

Just so you know who's behind this project, we're providing you with a bit of detail about our backgrounds.

---

**Jon Juffs, C.E.T., ACCI**
**Manager, Building Science**
**AME Materials Engineering**

 At AME Jon is responsible for a variety of projects including reserve fund studies, investigations, condition assessments, repair & replacement designs, contract administration, litigation support, expert reports, and research into improved building performance and capital planning procedures. AME is part of the Aecon Group, Canada's largest publicly traded architectural and engineering construction firm (TSE: ARE).

Since the late 1980s Jon's continuous employment has included technical and management positions with architectural and engineering companies, the Ontario Ministry of Housing and Municipal Affairs, and a water and sewer contractor.

Jon has become accustomed to preparing 80 to 100 reserve fund studies annually and he estimates that in all, he has prepared over 750 reserve fund studies and updates. Part of his experience includes reviewing over 600 other studies and preparing analyses and projections based on them. One such projection extrapolated from 450 data sources to a portfolio of 2,800 buildings with more than 57,000 residential units. The building types included high-rises, townhouses, walkup apartments, semi detached, and single family homes. His portfolio of work also includes capital repair planning and consulting for social housing providers, institutional assets, commercial holdings, and many individual condominium corporations.

Jon is a member of:

- Ontario Association of Technicians and Technologists
- Ontario Institute of Quantity Surveyors
- Professional Associate of the Canadian Condominium Institute
- CCI National Chapter Relations, Communications, and Finance Committees
- Canadian Condominium Institute – Huronia Chapter Director
- Association of Condominium Managers of Ontario Regional Expansion Committee

His ACCI accreditation, bestowed by the Canadian Condominium Institute, serves as recognition of having achieved a level of skill, professionalism, and knowledge of condominiums as it relates to certified engineering technology and reserve fund studies and planning that exceeds the already rigorous standards the Institute expects from its professional members. As an Associate of the Canadian Condominium Institute, Jon is recognized by clients and peers as standing out above the crowd.

Jon has, for some time, been actively sought after as a speaker at local and regional condominium conferences, and as a lecturer on specialized topics related to his areas of expertise. In the past five years he has presented individually and participated as a panel member at numerous conferences including Construct Canada, PM Expo, CCI, ACMO, and ONPHA.

If asked to sum up his approach to reserve fund planning, Jon says ... "It's not only the building science and engineering aspects that interest me, but knowing that well-prepared studies make community living better. After all, these are people's homes, and homes are more than a roof and walls or lofty curving stairs. It's a people-thing, in the end".

### Graham Oliver, B.Com.
### President, Oliver Interactive, Inc.
### Reserve Fund Aficionado

Graham Oliver is President of Oliver Interactive, Inc., a developer and marketer of proprietary software packages. The products are used in 23 countries around the world for determining optimal replacement times for industrial assets, and the proper intervals for replacement and repair. The mathematical models that underlie the calculations are those of Mr. Oliver's colleagues, the globally respected engineers Dr. Andrew Jardine of the University of Toronto and Dr. Nicholas Hastings in Australia.

Graham spent a great part of his working life at two respected organizations. He was with Du Pont for 19 years and served in various capacities related to marketing and market planning for its product lines. Subsequently he joined McGill University where he taught in the Faculty of Management and ran the Faculty's well-known Executive Institute, which offers seminars for high-level managers from all parts of Canada and the U.S. as well as from overseas organizations.

His academic teaching responsibilities were centered on Marketing Management, Marketing Planning and Sales Management, and he held classes for both graduate (MBA) students as well as undergraduate students.

His interest in property management stems from his serving for several years on the Board of his own condominium, and for one year as President. His insight into the management and organization of reserve funds required by condominiums, community associations and HOAs led to the development of a new software package called RFund reserve fund software. RFund is multi-featured but its principal purpose is to provide the means for Boards, Specialists and Property Managers to easily update their expenditure costs. By doing this, the near-term and long-term fund balances can be reviewed and funding plans adjusted as necessary. It helps keep reserve funds healthy.

Graham Oliver knows, as do many others, that too many co-owned properties pay too little attention to their reserves. As a result "horror stories" abound — inadequate balances are not foreseen, loans are required, special assessments are imposed — most of which could have been avoided with proper reserve fund management and control. It is scenarios like this that have led to the development of his company's software package, and to the co-authorship of this book. Graham's article, "Due Vigilance", on the need for continual updating of reserve plans, appeared in "Common Ground", the publication of the Community Associations Institute, in its November-December 2006 issue.

Footnote: As this is going to press, in late 2010, Graham's company is most of the way through the development of The Budget Machine, a new software product for the creation and management of properties' operating budgets. There's more detail on it in the pages that follow.

# Reserve Fund
## <u>Fundamentals</u>
### Part One

<u>Bringing Clarity to the Major Issues</u>
Our three-part "Fundamentals" chapter will take you, one step
at a time, through all the need-to-know elements of a property's reserve fund. New Board Members are our intended tar-
get. Professional providers — reserve planners and property
and community managers — will certainly be able to work more
easily with Boards that understand how their funds work.

Part One describes how the money in a reserve fund flows in,
and out.

---

How many times have we heard ... "Reserve fund methods,
principles and terms are really hard to grasp. The concepts,
the vocabulary ... it's all very confusing". It's a frequent
comment from those who are new to the area, and that would
include the tens of thousands of new Board Members who
get elected every year.

Our position is that it needn't be difficult to understand at all.
The methods and principles are not complicated, and the ter-
minology can be very easily translated into everyday language.

Having said that, we will now set out to try to prove what
we've just stated is true! This will be a short essay on the basic need-to-know fundamentals connected with reserve funds.
Here goes.

For now, think of a bank account, not a reserve fund. We'll build the bridge from one to the other, later.

You have an opening balance in your account at the beginning of May. If you were to visit the bank, that's the money you'd have in there, ready for you to use. You deposit money from various sources — the most common source is your pay from employment. After your deposit the balance in your account has grown. Then, you pay bills. With each payment, the balance gets a bit less. At the end of May, you've made deposits into your account, and you've taken payments out of the account (withdrawals) so your closing balance has changed. It becomes the opening balance for June.

Your balance is pretty healthy. You're not worried about "going under" — overdrafts. So you decide to take, let's say, $1500 out of the checking account and put it into a savings account to gain interest.

Your total personal funds now amount to the balance in your checking account *plus* the $1500 in your savings account.

Next month, you go through the same process. But you now have interest in your savings account so your money at the end of June is the total of your checking account, plus the amounts you have put into your savings account, plus the interest earned on the money in your savings account.

Let's move over to reserve funds. The elements covered on personal banking, above, are very similar. We'll talk in terms of a year now, instead of a month. Your reserve fund has a balance at the beginning of 2012 of $100,000. Every month, you collect fees from your unit owners. A portion of those fees is allocated for the payment of operating expenses — staff salaries, landscaping, electrical power, and so on. Another part of those fees is put into the reserve fund. The fees that are in the reserve fund are in "two parts" as well. Similar to our personal banking example, one part of the reserve fund money will be held in a checking account and another part will be put into interest-earning accounts.

Over the year you will pay a number of bills from the reserve fund account — from the fund's checking account, and (if required) from the fund's interest-earning account — to pay for major repairs and replacements in the building or on the property grounds.

If the total "money in" from fees and interest is greater than the "money out" that went to the contractors for labor and materials, your reserve fund balance will have grown. If your "money in" is less, you'll have a lower closing balance for this year than you began with. The next year's *opening* balance (for 2013) is, of course the same dollar-amount as the closing balance for 2012.

Pretty simple, right? And it doesn't get any harder!

Let's add a new dimension to the write-up. It's about planning ahead.

It's time to look at a few illustrative spreadsheets (tables). You'll find them at the end of this chapter.

Look for the spreadsheet with a "1" in a circle on the top line. Be sure to read the narrative above the table, and try to get a good picture of the expenditures data as shown on the table. Given the page-size it's not possible to show all the years across the sheet, nor is it possible to show all the components down the side of the sheet. But this small-size spreadsheet does, indeed, contain the same kind of data that a large one would contain.

Having finished the expenditures estimates, we'll turn now to the funding exercise — as we did with our cottage example. And once again, it's quite similar. Except that the amounts will be bigger.

With a co-owned property (condo, townhouse) you'd have an Opening Balance for the period you were planning for. Go to Spreadsheet 2 and you'll see the number 93 ($93,000)[2] as the opening balance in Year 1.

We added and subtracted amounts from the opening balance — we added $100 for funding (money in), and subtracted $80 for expenditures (the same number as in Spreadsheet 1). Thus we arrive at the closing balance for Year 1, $113 (93 + 100 − 80), which becomes the opening balance for Year 2.

And so on ... which means this process is repeated for every year of the funding plan.

---

[2] As we have noted in other chapters, we like to work in '000s, especially in our tables, for a number of reasons

Without regular contributions to the reserve fund from the unit owners, the fund would be depleted quite soon in most cases. So, in each year, you'll insert a dollar-amount that represents the funding you plan to collect from the owners.

This amount, of course, *would not include* fees collected for the property's non-reserve expenditures — usually called "operating" expenses. Our dollars here would be only the fees intended to pay for major repairs and replacements from the reserve fund.

You'd almost never be starting from scratch, because there would be a history of earlier funding levels. You'd see that last year, for example, you collected, say, $100,000. So perhaps as a trial balloon you'd want to plan for contributions at that level, for the next 30 years. (At this point in the process we're, quite rightly, ignoring inflationary effects).

So you put $100,000 into each year in each column (that is, each year) of your sheet. Doing this allows you to come up with the balances in each year. The Opening Balance plus the Funding amount, less the expenditures estimate, gives you a Closing Balance for each year, which is your Opening Balance for the next year. And so on.

We're going through this process step-by-step, and at this point, looking at spreadsheet 2 you'll see a negative balance in the final five years of the plan's span. In actuality you would probably never see this because our next step will have been done at the same time. The next step is to add in the interest earned on your invested funds.

Interest. For the cottage you could ignore it ... you're dealing with small numbers. But for a condo you cannot. Interest can represent a significant addition to the "money in" element of the plan. So there would have to be a row for the interest dollars as "money in". Here, you should look at Spreadsheet 3 and you'll see the row with interest figures in it. To get the interest dollars you'd estimate an interest rate and apply it to the balances in your reserve fund.

You might ask ... "apply it to which balance — (a) the opening balance for the year? ... (b) the closing balance for the year? ... (c) the average balance for the year?"

Actually, planners aren't consistent in regard to their choice. We like (c) the average balance for the year, but the arithmetic is a little harder. Not *really* hard, but trickier than using the opening balance (that's the easiest one). Our chapter on Investment Interest (page 79) covers this in more detail.

Before we leave the "Money In" elements — Owners' Contributions plus interest — let's just take a moment to refer to the Adequacy arguments in our chapter on that subject (page 29). You have to factor in the *acceptability* of the funding plan to the owners. For one thing, it will depend on their risk tolerances — the propensity to go for thin or thick cushions. For another, their attitude towards the property may vary from letting it deteriorate at an acceptable rate, or doing everything possible to maintain it in pristine, like-new condition.

So where are we? Let's look at Spreadsheet 3 again, and find out. On this sheet we have all the costs for each year — we'll

call it "money out" — and we have all our "money in" as well
... i.e., the funding dollars (owners' contributions). And now
we're adding in the interest dollars. We've got everything.
Everything we need to calculate all the annual opening and
closing balances in our fund. And the last row on Spreadsheet 3 reveals what these balances are.

Given our small-size spreadsheets, we cannot show you, in
this book, our complete Reserve Fund Plan for all of its 30
years. But we have produced one using RFund software. If
you e-mail us at book@oliver-group.com we'll send you a
copy by return e-mail. You'll see all the same figures, plus the
in-between numbers that we didn't have space for, plus a col-
orful chart of the entire plan.

When the balances are calculated you will note right away that
there are no longer any negative balances. (The interest took
care of that). You may, in many planning exercises, find that
your balances look too high or too low. That's when the real
fun begins. This is the time to "play" with the funding numbers — often called doing "what-ifs" — to arrive at balances
that are optimal. Neither too high nor too low. It's not hard
to do especially if you're using a computer spreadsheet or specialized reserve fund software[3].

This brings us to the end of Reserve Fund Fundamentals. For
more on funding methods see the chapter "Full Funding or
Cash Flow"[4]. Anything more you'd like to know? If so let us
know and we'll be delighted to provide you with a personal
reply.

---

[3] Please see our software chapter starting on page 137.
[4] This chapter begins on page 83.

The Reserve Fund Plan below shows the cost of repairs or replacements of various components over the 30-year span of the plan. This spreadsheet has been adapted for our book's page size limitation. Detailed component data for the 20 years between Year 5 and Year 26 is not shown here. The 20 Intervening Years panel provides the amounts for those 20 years. Please note that all figures are in '000s, and in "Today's dollars". As explained in the text for this chapter, no calculation has been applied for the effects of inflation.

| Component | 1 | 2 | 3 | 4 | 5 | 20 Intervening Years In Here | 26 | 27 | 28 | 29 | 30 |
|---|---|---|---|---|---|---|---|---|---|---|---|
| **Expenditures for 30 Future Years** | | | | | | | | | | | |
| Road Repairs | 3 | | | | | | 3 | | | | |
| Balcony Guards | | 30 | | | | | | | | | |
| Carpet Replacement | | | 18 | 18 | 18 | | | | 18 | 18 | 18 |
| Boiler Burner Replace | | | | | | | | | 5 | | |
| Boiler Replacement | | | 35 | | | | | | | | |
| Elevator Cab Refurbish | | | | 10 | | | | | | | |
| All remaining components | 77 | 20 | 37 | 12 | 82 | Total Expenditures over these 20 years total 2200 | 167 | 130 | 77 | 22 | 22 |
| **Total Expenditures** | 80 | 50 | 90 | 40 | 100 | | 170 | 130 | 100 | 40 | 40 |

❶

The Reserve Fund Plan spreadsheet continues below. The "Total Expenditures" figures have been copied from the preceding table. In this section of the plan we introduce some tentative Funding figures (owners' contributions), and by having an Opening Balance in Year 1 we are easily able to calculate the opening and closing balances in every year of the plan.

| Reserve Fund Plan for 30 Future Years | | | | | | | | | | | |
|---|---|---|---|---|---|---|---|---|---|---|---|
| | 1 | 2 | 3 | 4 | 5 | 20 Intervening Years In Here | 26 | 27 | 28 | 29 | 30 |
| Fund's Opening Balances | 93 | 113 | 163 | 173 | 233 | | 33 | 37 | 7 | 7 | 67 |
| Funding Schedule | 100 | 100 | 100 | 100 | 100 | Total Funding over these 20 years totaled 2000 | 100 | 100 | 100 | 100 | 100 |
| Total Expenditures | 80 | 50 | 90 | 40 | 100 | | 170 | 130 | 100 | 40 | 40 |
| Fund's Closing Balances | 113 | 163 | 173 | 233 | 233 | | —37 | 7 | 7 | 67 | 127 |

**②**

## Yours to Request

Would you like to see the complete set of figures?. You can obtain a copy, (and it includes color-coded charts as well), by simply sending us an e-mail. Address it to rfund@oliver-group.com.

We will reply with an e-mail attachment that supplies all the data and the charts.

The table that follows is identical to the table above, except that
we are now introducing one additional element ... interest earned.
Our preferred model is that interest is earned on the average of
the opening and closing balances in each year

| | Reserve Fund Plan for 30 Future Years | | | | | | | | | | | | |
| | 1 | 2 | 3 | 4 | 5 | 20 Intervening Years In Here | 26 | 27 | 28 | 29 | 30 |
|---|---|---|---|---|---|---|---|---|---|---|---|
| **Fund's Opening Balances** | 93 | 117 | 173 | 190 | 259 | | 203 | 140 | 115 | 120 | 186 |
| **Funding Schedule** | 100 | 100 | 100 | 100 | 100 | | 100 | 100 | 100 | 100 | 100 |
| **Interest Earned** | 4 | 6 | 7 | 9 | 11 | Total Interest over these 20 years totaled 133 | 7 | 5 | 5 | 6 | 9 |
| **Total Expenditures** | 80 | 50 | 90 | 40 | 100 | | 170 | 130 | 100 | 40 | 40 |
| **Fund's Closing Balances** | 117 | 173 | 190 | 259 | 270 | | 140 | 115 | 120 | 186 | 255 |

# Reserve Fund Plans
# Make 'em
# SMOOOTH

<u>A Good Plan is a Smooth Plan</u>
Making an effort to arrive at a smooth year-to-year expenditures schedule can really pay off. This chapter will reveal how bumpy repair and replacement programs can play havoc with funding issues. It's usually not possible to get your expenditures as smooth as a billiard table, but you'll get some hints that will take you part way.

---

### PART ONE — THE PRINCIPLES

Reserve fund plans, or studies, depict two main series of numbers. One of them is the expenditures forecast — the year-by-year estimates of the expected costs of major repairs and replacements for the plan-period. The other is the funding schedule — that's the series of annual dollar amounts contributed by unit owners as part of their monthly fees.

Of course there are the all-important balances as well, but the balances are derived from the two series mentioned above. Establishing and maintaining adequate balances is critical and many of this book's chapters address that challenge. But right now we're just going to talk about the expenditures and funding numbers.

Let's start with expenditures.

Your total estimated annual expenditures are derived from the sum of all the specific expenditures. For example, you may have for a given year, estimates for driveway paving at a cost of $25,000, central air conditioning replacement for $15,000, and some balcony restoration amounting to $55,000. So your total that year will be $95,000. All the other years have their own repairs and replacements and will add up to their own annual totals the same way.

It could happen though, (and it often does), that total annual expenditures will be "high" for a few consecutive years and "low" for a few consecutive years. If the annual expenditures were graphed, you'd have a line with significant peaks and valleys, as opposed to a flatter line. It would mean that your repairs are "bunched up" in some periods and at a low level in other periods.

If this is the case, you may have cause to re-think the expenditures plan. Here's why.

In the span of years where your expenditures are going to be high, you'll have reserve fund balances that become low and stay low until that period is over. Maybe you can get through it okay, but ... if you run into unexpected costs — a not unusual experience — your fund may be in trouble.

The other side of the coin is equally perilous. If you enter a period where your estimated expenditures are low, you'll run excessive balances for a while. Not good either, as you'll see.

So either way, you have a potential problem.

One way to fix the balances that get too low or too high is by raising or lowering the owners' contributions. Right? Yes, but that introduces another set of problems.

For one thing, owners prefer steady (or reasonably steady) monthly fees. They don't like to pay a lot for a while, and then pay a little for a while. So if you "use" the level of fees to level out the fund's balances, you'll get a flood of complaints.

Okay then. Why not just set the contributions (fees) at a high level and leave them there?

Not a good solution. In periods where expenditures are low the fund's balances will become excessive, and the owners will wonder why all that money is in the property's hands and not in their pockets, where it should be. And they would have a point!

The answer? It's found in the annual expenditures totals. If you have to work with a volatile expenditures series you'll run into the kinds of difficulties we've described. So the answer is to do as much as you can to level out the yearly expenditures estimates.

An approach that can do wonders to level out an up-and-down expenditures plan is to look at the possibilities of "staging" your repairs and expenditures. For example, consider the chances of refurbishing 25% of the balconies every second year, over eight years. For big jobs that must be done all at once — roofing would be typical — you would try to move other work out of the same timeframe.

Another idea: A greater level of detail in your components listings will enable you to schedule more "little jobs", and avoid big expenditures. For example, if, instead of having a line called Hot Water System you might break it down among boiler repair, coil replacements and so on.

Our suggestion is to do two things. Well ... do one thing first, and if necessary do the next thing. The first thing. Determine if you do, in fact, have an excessively variable series of annual expenditures. Usually just scanning a graph of them will give you the answer. But if you want to be sure, you will want to find out how your expenditures measure up on a smoothness index. The second part of this chapter goes into some detail on how the Condition Index is calculated.

The second thing. If your scan (or your index) says ... yes, your expenditures are too volatile, you can try some of the strategies we suggested above, to smooth them out. Trying what-ifs on a range of expenditure smoothings can ensure you'll end up with a good one[1].

Summarizing so far ... the benefits of putting time and effort into producing a plan with smooth expenditure and funding patterns is well worth it. A smooth plan really is a good plan!

---

[1] You will also find some tips on doing what-ifs in our software chapter (beginning on page 137), as well as more detail on the expenditures index.

## PART TWO — THE INDEXES[2]

The Condition Index is easily explained. If you have a plan that shows expenditures totaling a certain dollar amount over a 30-year period — say $3,000,000, or an average of $100,000/year, you would expect to see a normal 3-year period's expenditures amount to $300,000, i.e. 1/10 (10%) of the 30-year total. So the Condition Index takes the total for the 30-year periods, calculates the "moving-total" for every 3-year period, and describes the percentages. It is these percentages that make up the Condition Index of a property.

One qualifier. The Condition Index is actually these percentages *subtracted* from "100". A percentage of 10, (in this case a normal percentage) would show a Condition Index of 90 (100 – 10). Because of this "inversion" (turning 10% into an index figure of 90%), expenditure periods that are "going high" will appear as "lows" on the index chart. And expenditure periods that are "going low" will appear as "peaks" on the index chart.

We used expenditures in the example, above. The Funding Index calculation for contributions works exactly the same way.

The Condition Index tells you whether you have a smooth, or relatively smooth, expenditures plan. The Funding Index tells you whether you have a smooth, or relatively smooth, contributions plan.

---

[2] The plural of index, preferred by many people, is indices. Others prefer indexes. We flipped a coin and chose indexes. After all, the correct plural of condominium is condominia, isn't it?

English usage aside, we wish to acknowledge that the concepts of the Condition Index and the Funding Index were created by Gerald R. Genge Building Consultants Inc. (GRG) and used here with sincere appreciation by this book's authors.

To view a Condition Index Chart please contact us and we'll e-mail an example to you.

When you look at a Condition Index chart, if you see that most of the readings lie between 85 and 95 your expenditures plan is a very smooth one. We call it "optimal". If you see readings that are between 80 and 85 or above 95 you are in the "advisory" region. This is where you might take a second look at your expenditure plan to see if some of the variations can be smoothed. If you are under the 80% line, you are in the "Review your Plan" region. If you have readings in this region you should definitely look for ways to reduce the variations in your expenditures plan.

The index calculations and acceptability-zones are exactly the same for funding-plan improvements. The Funding Index chart is designed to tell you whether you have a smooth — (or relatively smooth) — contributions plan. That is, a plan where the owners' contributions do not change significantly from period to period.

# The Infrequency
## OF
# Reserve Fund Expenditures

Not a Lot of Work. Really!
Why are Boards and their professional advisors gun-shy about doing up-dates of their reserve fund numbers? We think it's because they believe it's a "lot of work". This chapter will show you that in reality, it isn't!

---

An under-recognized fact is that the number of expenditures per year from a property's reserve fund is very low. Would you believe ... less than one-a-month?

Of course some of them can be large when they happen, but the *number* of "projects" in any given year averages only 10.

It begs the question: Why is it, then, that so few Boards or Property Managers shrink from using their expenditure figures as updates to their existing reserve plans? Seems to us they're overlooking a heaven-sent opportunity to keep tabs on their ever-changing fund balances, and to spend very little time doing it.

Here's an example. Your plan calls for a carpeting job this year that is estimated to cost $40,000. The job gets done, as scheduled, but the Board decided to go with a better grade of carpeting and the job comes in at $52,000. (There's another issue regarding whether the Board should have upgraded the quality and exceeded the plan number, but that's a different matter). The estimated balance in the plan for the year, based upon the predicted costs, was (past-tense), $240,000. But now that the carpeting has been installed at a cost of $12,000 more than originally planned for, your end-of-year balance in the fund will be only $228,000. Plus ... all the ensuing balances, for every year in the plan, will be overstated by $12,000 as well.

Why not adopt a routine whereby you delete the estimated figures for jobs that are completed, and in their place, enter the actual figures. It's not a mammoth job — you only have to do it 10 times a year!

You agree? Fine. But exactly how do you do this?

If you're a Board member, one way would be to use the spreadsheet you received with your reserve plan. You would find the component that was repaired or replaced, cross out the estimated cost, enter the actual cost in its place, and recalculate the closing balance. A bit awkward? Yes, we think so.

For one thing, it would be hard to work with, especially once you had entered a number of up-dates. But the big problem would be that as a human, you could not possibly deal with the challenge of recalculating all the future balances. Maybe 30-years of them. So it's worse than "awkward". It's quite an unsatisfactory method.

Another way would be to ask your reserve planner for his computer file for the plan. You'd probably be given an Excel file, and you could use it to insert the real current figures when they occurred.

Still another suggestion is to use a software package that's designed expressly for this kind of work. Please see page 137. Dialog boxes will open up to accept your changes, graphs will illustrate what the effects of them are on your yearly balances, and all the other amounts will be re-calculated — interest, inflation, and so on.

You can use this software on your own computer, quite independently of the original work prepared by your planner. If you're not computer-savvy and don't want to get onto a keyboard at all, there are still some possibilities.

Perhaps your planner or property manager would take on the job. You might expect to pay a fee for this work. Or, since the software company itself offers the updating as a low-cost service item, consider using them. That way, you can sit back and receive the new outputs, and do hardly any work at all, beyond sending them your new actual expenditures data once in a while

Returning to our main point — the number of expenditures from your reserve fund, annually, are so few, that working them into your plan should be seriously considered. It's a sure way to keep your balances healthy and to avoid surprises that require drastic, and often costly, action.

# Immunizing
# Your
# Reserve Fund Plan

### Become Bulletproof

Being a Board Member or a Reserve Specialist has its rewards. For sure. But it has its downsides as well. The good news is that the downsides can be reduced, probably never to zero, but very close. This chapter offers a number of specific ideas for creating and maintaining a reserve fund plan that would be hard to criticize.

First, exactly what are we immunizing? Well, we're referring to immunizing your reserve fund plan. Preempting criticism of it. Ensuring that the preparers of the plan (most often Reserve Specialists), and the acceptors (most often the property's Boards) — can hold their heads up high.

It is not about immunizing the fund itself. That is, guaranteeing that the balances are adequate, that you won't run into a deficit position, or that it calls for excessive owner contributions. These are important challenges that we treat separately in other chapters.

So, how do you guard against criticism, or worse? "Worse" means being public embarrassment, not being re-engaged for the duties you were performing, or asked to go into some other line of work.

Here are a few suggestions that will help.

- o   Make sure your spreadsheet's opening balance for the projected years, starts with the very best number obtainable.
- o   Be certain that your plan lists all the possible repairable and replaceable components of the property.
- o   Get your repair or replacement intervals right.
- o   Use all possible sources to get the information you need on timing and costs.

Let's take a look at these questions, one at a time.

**Your spreadsheet's opening balance for the projected years must start with the very best number obtainable** — given recent expenditure and funding activity. To explain … if the first year of your 30-year plan starts in 2012, you will have an opening balance for 2012 which is identical to the closing balance for 2011 (the year you're currently in). But Year 2011 was not over when the plan was put together.

What you must do then, is obtain the latest monthly closing balance, and calculate as exactingly as you can what the funding dollars, the interest-earned dollars and expenditure dollars will be for the remaining months. That way you can arrive at a closing balance for 2012 that will make an unassailable foundation for all the figures that follow.

Balances "roll" forward. If the beginning balance is wrong, the reserve fund's projected balances for the entire 30-year plan will be out of whack.

**Be certain your plan lists all the possible repairable and replaceable components of the property.**

Components — these are the things that you as a community use and look after. They can be called capital assets, common elements, physical components, or corporate property. They are usually listed as rows down the margin of your plan. Make sure that everything on your property that can be repaired or replaced is listed and that you actually can locate everything that's listed. Also check to see if each component listed is really common to everyone or if it's the property of an individual unit owner. Appliances can be troublesome for example, so check your documents and plans carefully. This needs to be very accurate — your plan will be wrong if your components list[1] is wrong.

**Get your repair and replacement intervals right.**

How long is each component expected to last? Well, nothing lasts forever. Even the world's greatest monuments are being repaired and restored. All components are subjected to temperature variations, moisture changes, physical use, natural weathering, wear-and-tear, or structural loading. They're going to deteriorate. Some components simply become redundant, unused, or useless. So they don't require periodic refurbishing. Deciding on the correct intervals for replacement or repair can be very difficult in some instances; however, don't expect your shingles to last 40-years when every other shingle in your locale was replaced in 15- to 20-years.

Yes, an important characteristic of reserve fund plans is the *intervals* that are chosen between periodic repairs or replacements. If the building is quite new, and not many repairs or

---

[1] This book offers a list of over 400 components that may help. See page 128.

replacements have been carried out, the intervals you choose will be those recommended by the professionals you engage. Their experience with other properties will be transferred to the work they do for you. If you're one of the acceptors of their plan, don't hesitate to look over these intervals and question your planner regarding his or her recommendation.

If your property has been in existence for a while you should have records of when and how often work was done. You'll see that your last carpeting installation occurred 9 years after the previous installation, so (unless you've changed the quality-level of the carpeting) you can probably use that 9 years as your interval over the span of the plan for carpet replacements. We think that recent, *real* information is better than "standard estimates" that are often tempting to use.

**Use all possible sources to get the information you need on timing and costs.**
Now here's a challenge. Just where does one go to obtain realistic timing and cost estimates for replacement and repairs? One idea ... take a look at some published public tender results. The price your municipality paid for roofing, per square foot, for example. These tenders all work the same way — they say ... "give us your best price for these exact-same services or products". Rarely is there just one bidder, and almost never are there two bidders that come up with the same price. Sometimes the low bidder is one-quarter the price of the high bidder! Is the lowest bid the right one? Judging from the number of projects with cost over-runs, that doesn't seem likely.

Another source of information would of course be the professionals you'd call in to actually do the job — suppliers, contractors, and engineers. Get them to give you estimates for free by asking for "order-of-magnitude" numbers. They're good enough, and they can be used to compare one supplier's thinking with another's. If you're getting a few of them to respond, you will be deemed to have done a pretty thorough job. Consider, as well, using the estimate that's on the high side. That way you'll automatically build an element of conservatism into your plan.

Finally, talk to your neighbors. Ask what their experiences have been on their intervals and costs for major jobs. You can try using an extrapolation — (You would extrapolate by adjusting for the number of units and the square footage differences) — from a neighbor's low-bid, but be careful to build in a plus-factor for the possibility that yours will be higher. It's better to plan for the worst and hope for the best rather than the other way 'round.

To conclude, we're suggesting four areas where homework pays off. Homework that can be trotted out to demonstrate that you, as a Reserve Planner, or as a Board of Directors, have taken a number of steps, and have put in some real effort to ensure that your plan numbers are as good as they can get. Most people get their flu shots each year. Try our kind of immunization as well, to protect you from the unwelcome effects of disapproval from your community of unit owners.

# Reserve Funds.
# What Does
# "Adequate"
# <u>Really Mean?</u>
## Part One
## THE PEOPLE ISSUES

<u>Adequacy defined. Finally!</u>
One hears a lot about adequacy. But our impression is that it's most often used like patriotism and motherhood. You must believe in it, although exactly what you believe in may not lend itself well to being defined. This is about to change. This chapter begins by looking at some people–related influences on the definition of adequacy. Then we move onto something very exciting and very new. It addresses the question of adequacy as a quantitatively definable amount, and it has the potential to become recognized as a "first" in applying a truly scientific approach to the subject.

---

What does "Adequate" really mean? You know what? We were not all that sure, either! It's one of the most difficult questions there are, in regard to reserve fund balances. You've all heard "beauty is in the eye of the beholder". Well, so is adequacy.

Go into that new sandwich shop with a friend and order BLTs. He looks at his, and says ..."Wow, I'm not sure I can eat all that". You look at yours and you say ... "Shucks, this isn't enough to feed a canary". What one diner sees as more than adequate, the other sees as less than adequate.

Well, we, your co-authors, think setting standards for adequacy in reserve funds is a little more scientific. Okay, maybe it isn't yet, but it soon may be. Why? Because we have spent many long hours, have looked at literally hundreds of reserve plans, argued about the merits of various formulas, and ... we are going to offer some objective sets of rules, models, and indicators that bring some science and logic to bear on the adequacy question[1].

We're going to unveil these approaches in Part Two of this chapter. Right now we're going to concede that there's still a subjective element to settling on the so-called adequacy level of a property's reserve fund balances, and it probably has a lot to do with risk aversion versus risk acceptance (or tolerance, if you prefer). Nevertheless, in Part Two we're going to provide you with real specific tools that will help you determine the adequacy of your reserve fund balances.

You see, creating a Reserve Fund Plan that takes the predicted expenditures and sets up a funding schedule to cover the expenditures isn't all that difficult. You can, and would, use funding numbers such that no years in the plan show a predicted balance of less than zero. The question is, however, how much *above* the zero-line should you plan to reserve? This is where the personalities and politics get interesting.

The risk *averse* will say ... "I don't ever want to see this property having to announce a special assessment to cover major expenditures. They should be planned for, and funded with

---

[1] We might as well say, right now, that this is our answer to those that say the Full Funding approach automatically takes care of adequacy. They believe that because you can say "our property is 83% funded", it actually means something. Well, it doesn't. For one thing they believe that 57% funded is all right! Read our chapter on this on page.83.

regular contributions, over time". They'd say the same thing about taking out loans, we're sure. So they'd insist on a thick "cushion" in case expenditures came in at higher levels than expected, or in case the repairs were needed sooner than expected. And this will happen sometimes, for sure. That's the time you'll get a lot of "I told you so" remarks.

All right, almost everyone will agree that some cushion is necessary[2]. But the risk *tolerators* will say — "We don't want our money tied up in the reserve fund, we want it in our pockets". They would add that getting a loan or having a special assessment really doesn't bother them all that much. Besides, they'd say, "We may move some day, and all that excess money we put into the reserve fund won't be refunded. It will be in there for the benefit of the people that still live here".

The cushion, for these people, the risk tolerators, would be thin. The cushion for the risk avoiders would be thicker.

So the question comes down to, perhaps — what is the thickness of the cushion that will be acceptable to most of the risk averse crowd as well as to the risk tolerant crowd?

To answer this question, we're going to leave the "behavioral" discussion to look at some numbers-based indicators that can put an objective face on the problem. You'll understand this better once we get into the subject. And that will happen in Part Two of this chapter on Adequacy.

---

[2] Please see our chapter on "Your Reserve Fund's Shock Absorbers", page 102, for more on this.

# Part Two
## THE ADEQUACY RATIOS METHOD

Part One of this chapter on adequacy focused mostly on the difficulties of dealing with the mind-sets of two different kinds of people — those who are risk tolerant and those who are risk averse.

In this section, we're going to provide real indicators that will, at the very least, help to identify whether a reserve fund plan is, indeed, healthy (even "too" healthy!), or in peril.

Your authors have carried out a great deal of original research by looking at many properties' actual reserve plans, and we've reached some conclusions and arrived at some methods that in our opinion can almost certainly help planners or boards to decide whether their planned fund balances are all right, or not.

For each property, we added up the funding dollars of all the contributions over all the plan years. And we added up the expenditure dollars over all the plan years. We did the same with the total closing balances of the fund.

Essentially we looked at two ratios that represent the Adequacy Ratios Method. One ratio — the Adequacy Directional Ratio, indicates if, during the life of the plan, your balances are heading north (good) or heading south (not-so-good). The other ratio is the Adequacy Confidence Ratio which indicates if, over the life of the plan, the balances are sufficient (or insufficient, as the case may be), to cover the expenditures from the plan with a reasonable cushion for the unexpected repairs and replacements that are expected to occur.

The Adequacy Directional Ratio (ADR) is derived by dividing the total of all the monies going into the fund over the plan period (owners' contributions plus earned interest), by all the monies going out of the reserve fund over the plan period. If you have an ADR of 1:1 you'd be neither going north nor south. If you have an ADR of 1.2 to 1 you'd be going north — over the plan period you would have more money going into the fund than coming out. If your ADR was 0.7 to 1 for example, you'd be heading south. Not so good, unless your reserves were overly conservative, and you wanted to bring them down to more acceptable levels.

That's the ADR, the Adequacy Directional Ratio. How about the ACR, the Adequacy Confidence Ratio?

It's derived by totaling all of the closing balances over the plan period, and totaling all of the expenditures over the plan period, and dividing the balances total by the expenditures total. If your ratio were "6", you would have, on the average, six times as much money in the fund at any given time, than the money you'd require for a typical year's repairs and replacements. With a ratio of "6", we believe you'd be in good shape, by the way. Your cushion might not take care of every possible catastrophe or unexpected breakdown imaginable, but it would certainly take care of most of them, by far.

Having said that, it can get a wee bit more complicated. Funds may have a different Adequacy Ratios in the beginning years of their plan than the latter years of their plan. And this should be examined as well.

Let's say you divide your plan years into a span for the first third of the years (say, the first 10 years of a 30-year plan), and the remaining two-thirds of the years — the last 20 years. We've found, in the plans we examined that there's a pretty consistent tendency for the ACR to be lower in the first part of the plan, and higher thereafter.

The reason, we believe, is that to get to a higher ACR in the early years, the funding dollars would have to be higher than many of the owners would like to pay. So, to avoid the un-pleasantness of heated debates, boards will recommend fund-ing levels that won't be as controversial as higher ones. They "whistle past the graveyard" so to speak.

Well, all right. It's true that jacking up the contributions sud-denly can be irritating, and maybe getting the first few years to an ACR of 4 would indeed be a hardship. But at the very least the facts should be *recognized* for what they are, and some steps should be taken to begin corrective action.

The Adequacy Directional Ratio could come in handy here as well. If you applied it to the first one-third of your plan, you could immediately see that perhaps you were heading North but not at the rate that your finding required. So instead of an ADR of 1.2 you could try something higher to get it onto a more northerly heading.

The point here is that both of these ratios are useful in their own right, and they're sometimes even more useful when one of them is used to improve the other.

The foregoing material covered our Adequacy Ratios Method for determining if your plan, over your plan's span, will have sufficient funds to pay for the anticipated expenditures. If your plan meets the ACR criteria, you'll be all right, overall. But ... while your funding may be adequate overall, some years may have balances that appear a bit low. Low meaning that if unexpected repairs are required at that time you might not be in good enough shape to easily cover them.

So ... should we not also have a *minimum* for our year-by-year closing balances then? We think so. We suggest this as a Minimums Rule.

> **Your plan's yearly closing balances should not be below the average annual expenditure of all the years in the plan[3].**

That way, you'd be very safe. We'd even say that you could allow up to three years' balances to fall below the calculated minimum, but we'd say it with a few qualifications. Take the minimums rules more seriously if —

o   The years that fall below the minimum level are sequential years, or even just close, in time to each other.

o   The years that fall below the minimum are way out in the future. You'll have plenty of time to tweak them in future plans.

o   You cannot re-arrange your expenditures enough to ensure that the below-minimum

---

[3] If you are more risk-averse, you could change the "average annual expenditure" to 1.5 times or 2 times the average annual expenditure.

years' balances get boosted enough to put them over the minimum level.

Leaving our Adequacy Ratios for a moment, let's go to still another set of guidelines for adequate funding. We have two quick rules-of-thumb that address the question of "minimums" — minimum balances and minimum funding levels.

The first one says — a condo property should probably assess the funders a minimum of $80-to-$100 per unit per month. That'll bring in $96,000-to-$120,000 per year in a 100-unit property. This figure reflects the dollars going towards the reserve fund only of course, and not the dollars going towards the operating budget.

Another one ... a condo property should attempt to plan for annual closing balances that are never lower than $500 per unit. Thus a 100-unit building would see minimum closing balances of $50,000 over the span of its reserve fund projections.

Interestingly, a townhouse will normally run with lower balances and lower assessments than a high-rise condo, because it does not have many of the replaceable and repairable components that a high-rise does. (Elevators, for example).

Further, the economic status of the property will also have a bearing. An up-market property will demand more in the way of impeccable upkeep than a less prestigious one. These are fairly rough guidelines. We'd like to do more research on the kinds of ranges one might expect under various assumptions.

When we do, we'll publish our findings of course, and share them with our readers.

There you have it. Three easily-applied answers, in this chapter, on calculating adequate yearly balances in your reserves plan, determining if your funding is getting better or getting worse, and even ensuring that all or most of the year's balances are acceptable. Here's to commendable planning practices!

# Part Three

The table below will allow you to pinpoint "where you are" in terms of the confidence you can have in your funding adequacy. Essentially, you will have <u>diagnosed</u> your plan.

| The Adequacy Confidence Ratio [Closing Balances over Expenditures] | | |
|---|---|---|
| | **For the First Third Of the Plan Span** | **For the Remainder Of the Plan Span** |
| | **N O R M S**<br>Low ACR    Zero to <2<br>Middle ACR  2 to <8<br>High ACR    8 and over | **N O R M S**<br>Low ACR    Zero to <3<br>Middle ACR  3 to <6<br>High ACR    6 and over |
| **1** | Low | Low |
| **2** | Low | Middle |
| **3** | Low | High |
| **4** | Middle | Low |
| **5** | Middle | Middle |
| **6** | Middle | High |
| **7** | High | Low |
| **8** | High | Middle |
| **9** | High | High |

**The table, above**, includes a column for each of two sections of a reserve plan — the fist third of the plan and the remainder. Our research revealed that the ratio of fund balances to anticipated expenditures are typically different in the early years when compared with the later years. The norms then are not the same, so for a better handle on the adequacy of your property's balances it's therefore better to look at these two time-periods separately.

The nine rows are designed to have you pinpoint your ACR situation so that we can offer the right prescription for further action. For example, you may find you have an ACR of 4.3 in the first third of your plan, and an ACR of 6.7 for the remainder. According to the norms you have middle ACR for the first part of your plan and a high ACR for the remainder. A middle-high combination. That's in row 6. You would then go to the Nine Prescriptions on the next page, and examine our prescription Number 6.

Once you have determined the <u>treatment</u> that's required (if any) to bring your plan into a confidence-range that is satisfactory, our Adequacy Directional Ratios (ADRs) will indicate

## The Adequacy Directional Ratio
### [Funding over Expenditures]
Funding includes all money in — funding plus reserve fund interest

| For the First Third Of the Plan Span | For the Remainder Of the Plan Span |
|---|---|
| **NORMS**<br>Low ADR    Zero to <1.1<br>Middle ADR    1.1 to <1.3<br>High ADR    1.3 and over | **NORMS**<br>Low ADR    Zero to <1.0<br>Middle ADR    1.0 to <1.2<br>High ADR    1.2 and over |

if your funding schedules in each of the span ranges — first third, and remainder — will work to bring your ACRs into line with your new, more satisfactory confidence levels.

Similar to the ACRs, we have also developed norms for the ADRs.

# The Nine Prescriptions

These Low, Middle and High ADR ranges will be referred to in the points that follow. The numbers for the paragraphs refer to the numbers in the first column of the ACR Table.

1    Your ACR is low throughout the entire span of your plan. Look at your ADR numbers. It's likely they are in the lower range as well. To improve your ACRs in both parts of the span, you should improve your funding plans. You will almost certainly need to plan for ADRs in the high range — 1.3 or higher — for the first third of your plan, and in the high range or the middle range for the remainder of your plan.

2    Your ACR is low in the early years, and is in the middle range in the remaining years.

Action to improve your funding is required now to get your ACRs for early years into better shape. Use a high-level ADR — 1.3 or higher. This may be enough to provide satisfactory ACR levels in the remaining years. If not, continue using high-range (or middle-range) ADRs in the remaining years as well.

3    You have good funding numbers in the last two-thirds of your plan but your confidence ratio is low in the immediate future. Increase you funding to an ADR of 1.3 or better in the first third of your plan. This might have enough of a carry-through effect to allow funding in the middle ADR range — 1.0 to 1.2 — for the remaining years.

4    You have a middle-range ACR in the first third of your plan. This middle range is quite wide however. It runs from 2 to 8.

If you're in the lower part of it you cannot be quite as confident as if you were in the upper half of it. In this case, try to improve your ACRs in both parts of your plan ... the early third, and the last two-thirds. You will almost certainly need to plan for ADRs in the high range for the first third of your plan, and in the high range or the middle range for the remainder of your plan.

If you're in the upper part of the middle ACR you can be more confident about the early part of your plan. But you still must deal with your low ACR in the remainder of your plan. Increase your annual funding dollars gradually beginning about 5 years before the last third of your plan commences. Aim for an ADR of 1.3 or better in this period. This way it will be a relatively painless escalation and will contribute towards an improvement in the ACR for the last two-thirds of your plan.

5   Your ACRs are in the middle-range throughout your plan. However, as noted in No. 4 above, the middle range is quite wide however. If you're in the lower part of it, the suggestions in No. 4 still hold true, although you can work with middle range ADRs in the latter half of your plan.

If you're in the upper part of the middle range, you can be quite confident that your plan is funded adequately.  But remember that actual expenditures frequently vary from planned expenditures, so calculate your Adequacy Ratios every time you up-date your expenditure numbers.

6   You only have to concern yourself with the first third of your plan span, and then only if the ACR is in the bottom half of the middle range for this period.  If it is, take immediate steps to improve your ADR for this part of your plan.

7   You're in great shape for the first third of your plan and in not as great shape for the remainder of your plan span.  The reason is almost certainly due to heavy expenditures that are planned for the last two-thirds of the plan.  You can probably get a medium (or even a high) ACR for the later years if you begin about 5 years prior to the beginning of the later years, to escalate your funding gradually.  Then, you can go into the later-years period more securely.  The biggest risk you will have (and it's not a bad risk to have) is getting your reserve fund excessively high.  So watch for ACRs that are over 6 — a little over is all right.  A lot over means your cushion is unrealistically high, and too much of your unit owners' money is in the fund rather than in their pockets.

8   You're sitting pretty. But review our suggestions in No. 7.  True, you don't have a problem in the first third of your plan, but you do have to be careful that you don't have an excessively high ACR in the remaining years.

9   Ditto.  See No. 8, please

---

# The Adequacy Ratios Method
# Its Specific Purpose

We've run into a particular question about our adequacy ratios that we think needs to be addressed for a better understanding of it.  We're asked ..."We create our reserve plans using tried-and-true systems like the Full-Funding Method or the Cash Flow Method that provide acceptable balances.  So why have a set of measurements like your adequacy ratios as well?  Aren't they simply redundant?"

Our answer is unequivocally "no".  Even "adequate" reserve plans range from quite "thin" to quite "fat".  But almost all of them can be described as acceptable. The components have been examined, the expenditures have been carefully calculated, there are no zero or negative balances, and so on. But how does your plan compare with others in the overall co-owned properties universe? Is it on the "thin" side, or the "fat" side? Is it among those that are top-of-the line ... robustly healthy and ready for almost all eventualities, or is it in the lower echelons where you're living closer to the edge?

That's where our adequacy ratios shine! They deliver information that says you're in the top third meaning that 2 out of 3 properties don't measure up to your standards. You're among the "winners". Or they say your plan is "okay" ... could be better, could be worse. Or our ratios signal that your plan is "iffy" and should probably be improved.

The Full Funding and Cash Flow Methods provide acceptable balances in the absolute sense, but the adequacy ratios offer a look at the relative quality of your balances compared to all other properties. They're definitely worth the effort. For more ... see our Funding chapter on Page 83.

# Reserve Funds
# The Precision Fallacy

<u>Making Life Less Complicated</u>
Not everyone will be convinced that numbers to the umpteenth decimal place should be banned. But if our arguments make sense to you, you could end up with much more intelligible reserve fund plans, with no appreciable downside at all.

---

"Don't use a scalpel, when a meat-axe will do". Kind of a grisly expression, right? But its message is right on. It speaks to the quite common confusion between precision[1] and usefulness. Not to mention that unnecessary precision can consume a lot more time, effort and money for no improvement in results.

This chapter is all about the fairly common belief that exact-looking numbers are somehow "better" than round numbers. Or that being "out" a little bit from the exact answer will somehow lead to all kinds of unwanted consequences.

How tall are you? Let's say you're 5' 11". Would it make you feel better to know that you're really 5' 11.215784"? How far is your office from your home? 8½ miles? Actually, it's really 8.375921 miles. Aren't you glad we corrected that?

---

[1] Your authors, like most human beings don't agree on absolutely everything. For example, JHJ is convinced that "precision" is the word that best fits our chapter — its title and its content. GDO likes "accuracy" better. (One dictionary indicates that "precision" is simply a higher order of "accuracy". Another source sees them as different than one another). JHJ won the coin-toss so we've used JHJ's word, mainly, but we also sneaked "accuracy" in a couple of times.

Turning to reserve funds, we see a lot of reserve fund plans on spreadsheets that give the yearly balances as $457,704, $2,750,312 and $87,432. Ask yourself — would you really have less confidence in the plan if those figures were exhibited as $458, $2750, and $87 with a little note saying ... all figures rounded to the nearest thousand?

We hope your answer is "No", and if it is, you'd be solidly in our camp today! Round numbers are an *improvement* over "exact" numbers, not the other way around. For one thing, the plan looks better. Less ink, faster to comprehend, not as formidable-looking. Book publishers and magazine publishers know that when their material is more attractive it gets improved readership. It even gets better comprehension. People grasp the trends and the highs-and-lows better, and a lot more quickly. Your unit owners will appreciate that.

Let's turn, though, to examples where even the rounded figure does not tally with someone's idea of what it should be. Well, if it were a bank document, or an investment total, we'd agree that it should be investigated, or fixed. But we're talking here about a reserve fund <u>plan</u>. *Projections* of future events. They're estimates of *potential* occurrences, not historical reality.

Please don't misinterpret this. We believe 100% in planning, and we believe a plan should be, in the end, as close to actual future occurrences as it's possible to make it. But we also believe that nothing predicted for the future ever turns out to be exactly as forecast. To think otherwise, is just, well ... delusional.

Having said that, what lessons can be applied to reserve fund spreadsheets?

To answer this, let's take a real example that we've run into. It has to do with the interest the fund earns on its invested balances. Reserve Fund Planners use different mathematical models to calculate it. (This is covered in some detail in our chapter that begins on page 79, "Reserve Fund Investment Interest"). Using these different models will result in interest dollars that are not the same as one another's. (And this even assumes that the interest *rates* they have chosen are the same for everyone). So, if Planner A does your Plan you'll get a certain set of numbers for interest, and if Planner` B does your Plan you'll get another set of numbers. People might ask — "Who's right? Which set should we accept?"

The answer is — they're both right! For one thing the interest figures are usually small compared with the expenditure and funding figures, so no matter what they are (within limits) it doesn't matter. For another thing if you took the total interest dollars they calculated for any 3- or 4-year span, the total interest dollars would be nearly identical, so in the end you're not overstating or understating the interest earnings.

Yet ... (and this is our theme for this chapter), there would be people that would say, "These figures can't be accurate". Our answer is, they're not supposed to be "accurate" — the Plan itself isn't "accurate", it's a plan for heaven's sake, not a measurement. Plans are supposed to reflect a reasonably good picture of what the reserve fund interest will add up to in future years. And the plans would do that, even if the dollars appear to be "out" here and there.

Remember, we're talking about variations — (due to rounding or due to using a different interest formula) — that result in some "inexactness" in the order of 1%, 2% maybe 3%. Far less (repeat: *far* less) than the inexactness that's inherent in the predictions for the dollar costs of the repairs and replacements themselves. Not to mention the timing of them! The expenditures are the big numbers — the ones that need to be as right as humanly possible. You hear people say ... "Don't sweat the small stuff", and we agree wholeheartedly. Get them as right as possible[2], and then, move on.

To conclude, this whole chapter was engendered by a Reserve Fund Specialist telling us that a certain spreadsheet setup did not conform to "generally accepted accounting principles"! Sort of like saying, "a giraffe doesn't conform to the generally accepted appearance of a zebra". Don't tell anybody, but hey, it's not *supposed* to.

---

[2] See the chapter "Immunizing Your Reserve Fund Plan" for more on this.

# Update
# Your Reserve Plan
# QUARTLERLY

<u>Quarterly?  Are you for real?</u>
Well, it depends on how you define update.  We are NOT suggesting that you should initiate a new reserve study every three
months.  Not at all.  We are suggesting however, that you use
real expenditure numbers to replace your plan-numbers for a lot
of very good reasons.  And we suggest you tackle this really
quite-undemanding routine every quarter.

---

The consequences of every single expenditure from your reserve fund are greater then you may think.  We don't mean
that the impact of spending money has suddenly become
more unpleasant — we already know that.  What we do mean
is that the information value of these real expenditures (as
opposed to planned expenditures) has real significance.  They
can be, and indeed are, significant in regard to the near and
long-term picture of your reserves balances.

Let's take the simple case where you have a predicted expenditure in this year's column of your plan for, say, $40,000 for
driveway repair and repaving.  Even though you have inflation
built into your plan, the cost of this kind of work has risen
much more, and it amounts, instead, to $55,000.

These surprises happen all the time.  You can almost bet on
the fact that several of the jobs you plan for at one expenditure amount are, when the time comes, actually going to cost
more.

The paving work, and some of the other greater-than-expected costs will all affect your reserve balances of course, So when it comes time for a new reserve study the balance in the fund is not what it was re originally predicted to be. If it's lower (and it usually will be) your planner will have to suggest a schedule of increased owner contributions to bring them back up to scratch. You will have been, essentially, "blindsided" by the newly-revealed fact that your fund deteriorated behind your back, so to speak.

It needn't have happened. If, as expenditures were made, you had worked with the plan spreadsheet and replaced the plan-numbers with the actual dollars as they arose, you'd be on top of your reserves outlook and you would have acted sooner to make a course-correction. You would not have "hit the iceberg".

This doesn't imply that you wouldn't have spent those larger amounts. Likely, that couldn't have been avoided. But you'd have seen the consequences earlier and you'd have had the opportunity to make incremental changes to your funding requirements. Small changes are always more tolerable than sudden, large changes.

We suggest you pull the invoices together on a quarterly basis to update your plan. It slices the job up into little bits and doesn't become a big project. But most importantly, it keeps you current at sensible intervals that are not too long or too short. To repeat: quarterly.

Towards the end of this chapter we're going to suggest *how* this can easily be done. But first let's look at another phenomenon of expenditures.

## Reserve Fund Expenditures
## Are Not Isolated Events

So far, we've learned that substituting the real expenditure, which is $20,000 higher than the planned one, is a good thing to do. That simple substitution will affect the fund's future balances right across the board ... for 30 years. And rightly so.

But there's a bit more to it. Let's go on a bit with other meaningful chain effects that our carpeting replacement is causing.

For one thing, the driveway cost $15,000 more than you expected. If, in your reserve fund plan, you have a driveway repaving job in there every 12 years, perhaps all those estimates are low as well. The chances are very good they are, because your planner was thinking $40,000, not $55,000[1].

So here you are with a plan that shows a replacement cost of $40,000 at least twice (every 12 years) in the driveways row of the spreadsheet, when it should be showing $55,000. Imagine what that variance is doing to your projected balances. It's showing them artificially too high because the expenditures are, incorrectly, too low. And the error is increasing as you go through the plan's span.

There's more.

---

[1] We're referring to uninflated dollars in these examples. Reserve plans are best created using today's dollars, with an extra "edition" showing inflated values as well.

Suppose that instead of the current replacement occurring in the year that it was planned for, this replacement is taking place 2 years ahead of time. That can happen. The replaced carpet just didn't stand up for as long as expected. The plan called for an eight-year interval and you replaced it after only six years.

Your plan, however, is showing carpet replacement expenditures occurring every eight years. If you adjust the plan (as you should) you'll have the costs occurring every six years. What a difference it will make to your projected balances a few years out!

Our point is that a single expenditure from the fund can, and does, have broad and costly (and compounded) implications.

All right, how do you handle this? As in our initial example, you adjust your plan as real expenditures occur. We suggest doing it quarterly. You adjust the carpeting replacement dollars not only for the single actual expenditure dollars being different than the estimate, but you adjust it also for the probability that later on, similar expenditures will resemble the latest real expenditure and not the earlier planned *amounts*. You also adjust your plan for the change in the *interval* if you think the planned interval now looks too long, given your latest experience.

To recap, you must use your expenditure information *as it comes in* to adjust your plan quarterly. Three kinds of info — (1) expended dollars that are different than planned for … (2) the replacement being required in a different year than expected (which affects the years that all the subsequent replacement will be made), and …(3) the fact that the interval between replacement may not be the same as it was in the original plan.

If you do all that, your future balances will be significantly closer to what you can really expect in the years ahead.

## How Do You Do All this?

All reserve plans are created on a spreadsheet. That's a large table with the years across the top and, among other things, the property's components down the side. The predicted expenditures are slotted into to each little square (cell) that's available for each year and for each component. When each year's expenditure's columns are totaled, you have a row of total expenditures for each year along the bottom of your spreadsheet.

This row of expenditures is combined with other numbers — the funding dollars and earned interest amounts — to arrive at yearly reserve fund balances. The balances in one year, of course, are dependant on the balances in the previous year. So any change in any one single year will affect the reserve balances for all the remaining years of the plan.

Fortunately we're blessed with computer software that will accept a change in one year and make the adjustments in that year as well as in all the subsequent years, in a fraction of a second. We won't go into software here but if you'd like you can contact us to learn more.

Still, even with this marvelous software there is a need to think carefully about the consequences of each expenditure in regard to the kind of impact it will have on your plan. Whether the new expenditure data will affect only one year (and by how much), whether it will necessitate adjustments to expenditures in future years and whether the interval between the particular expenditure should be changed — all of these must be handled properly as input into the spreadsheet's cells.

Again, happily, we have an answer. To make the decisions we talked about above, we have a simple Expenditure Decision Expeditor (EDE) to offer to you (free of course) that will guide you to the right answers. It's not designed to fit the format of this book but we'll send it to you as a WORD document if you send an e-mail to us[2].

Not only does the EDE greatly assist you to properly arrive at the correct changes to your plan, (the correct amounts and timing), but it also allows you to add notes regarding the reasons for the changes. This information is invaluable to your reserve planner when a new study is being prepared.

One more word, if we may, on the EDE. It's designed not only to guide you towards the correct adjustment to make to your plan, but it also provides for a section of "relevant notes". These notes will form a record of exactly what changes were made and why they were made. It's an invaluable log of reserve fund expenditures and the reasons for them. Without a doubt, your planner will be ecstatic about having these notes when the next reserve study rolls around.

The foregoing addressed the matter of how these changes can be made. Another question concerns "who" should do them.

---

[2] Contact us at rfund@oliver-group.com

With the proper tools (Excel or RFund software) the Board can do these themselves. On the other hand your reserve planner or property manager might be persuaded to do it. Maybe for a fee, may not … it would be up to you and your provider to work it out. We can tell you though that most properties average only two or three reserve fund expenditure payments each quarter so it's not by any means a huge workload.

You may note that we, ourselves, can handle this updating for you, as a service. Economically. We call it our "Reserve Plan Assurance Program", and we'll tell you all about it if you'd like to contact us.

Before closing this chapter let's not forget the big picture. That is … your reserve plan should not be a static document that's revised every few years and then gets filed away until the next time. It's a living breathing document that, when used properly (and often) can keep your fund in great shape and avoid unexpected assessments and loans for balances that "unexpectedly" begin to fall short.

P.S. Please turn the page for a bit more.

**ADDENDUM**

# Our 81mg Analogy

We often refer to the "health" of a reserve fund — *creating* a healthy plan, *keeping* it healthy, and so on. That's why we liked the suggestion of a reader who remarked that our oft-mentioned exhortations to continually update your plan sounded a lot to her like the new, and very effective aspirin therapy.

We're talking about taking one 81mg small-dose tablet of aspirin a day to get significant protection against suffering a heart attack. Not only are the results proven, in study after study, but the regimen is not time-consuming, not complicated and not expensive.

Keeping on top of your reserves in the same way ... routinely employing an easy affordable and *regular* therapy can yield a significant pay-off as well.

Our "pill" is the updating routine which we discussed in most of this chapter. You might look at our "More Free Things" offer on page 55, also.

Updating regularly — say, quarterly — has everything going for it with no downside at all. That's why we like this medical, health-related analogy so well. Our feeling is that if you're dedicated to maintaining your personal health, you're probably also receptive to keeping your reserves in good shape too.

I think we'll change the old adage to ...

**81 milligrams of prevention**
**Is worth a kilogram of cure!**

VISIT
oliver-group.com/rfund
TO CHECK OUT OUR LIST OF

 # More Free Things

## LOTS OF VALUABLE GIVE-AWAYS
### LIKE

- A 400 item Components List
- Our Investment Log software
- Expenditure Decision Expediter
- Our Evaluate-Your-Plan offer
- Three available budget booklets
- How this book *can* be obtained free
- Our most-read chapter on updating
- How to Create a Plan from Scratch

### AND LET'S NOT FORGET
A Free 60-Day Trial of the real thing
RFund reserve fund software

NONE OF IT COSTS ONE CENT
NONE OF IT OBLIGES YOU TO DO MORE

# Reserve Fund Essentials

## Available in Quantity

How about getting copies of this book for everyone associated with your property

**All your Board Members, your Community/Property Manager, Reserve Specialist, and your Accountant**

### OUR PRICING* MAKES IT EASY!

Single Copies, each                    $24.95

2–5 Copies, deduct 10%

6 copies and more, deduct 15%

### ADD SHIPPING*
(Per book)

| | |
|---|---|
| Single Copy | $3.50 |
| 2 – 5 Five Copies | $1.80 |
| 6 Copies and more | $0.95 |

### ADD TAX
(Canadian Destinations)

Add 5% GST to the dollar total of book costs + shipping

FOR ADDIITONAL ORDERING DETAILS GO TO
oliver-group.com/book

* Prices for the book and for shipping are subject to change. Please visit the web link above for the latest prices before ordering

# Give Me A Break

<u>Oh, the shabby work some planners do</u>
Not ALL planners, by any means. Not even a LOT of planners. But SOME planners deliver reserve plans that are disgraceful. Maybe you have experiences of your own. But here are some of our discoveries — all chronicled with the intention of alerting everyone to the things that can, and do, happen.

---

When I see something outrageous in print, one of my oft-used expressions is ... "Give me a break!" Usually quickly-followed by ... "Can this be for real?" If the material is written by someone who *defines* it as speculation, or if the author discloses that he or she is not all that knowledgeable on a particular topic, that's fine, But when a report is delivered to a client, and the report writer has presented himself as an expert, that's something else.

Most reserve fund planners present themselves as experts. And many, indeed, are. They have credentials, they have carried out numerous studies, and they can cite clients' opinions that back up their satisfaction with their work. Others cannot demonstrate résumés that look as good, yet they may have what it takes to perform very well. None of us enter this world with experience. We'd guess, and it's only a guess, that you'd likely get a better study done by the first group than the second. But we would apply the same warning in regard to planners from both groups. That warning is ... flawed plans are created every day, and they emanate from so-called "veteran" specialists, as well as from less-experienced planners.

What kinds of flaws? Well ... here are a few. Some are caused by simple carelessness, but others may be deeper and reflect a shortage of some basic know-how. Error-prevalent arithmetic, plans that are difficult or next-to-impossible to understand, the inability to "see" underlying problems that another planner would investigate, numbers or property components that are left out, a scarcity of information that good studies usually include. And so on. These are the kinds of planners we should worry about since they can potentially cause a number of very serious problems for those that use their services.

We're going to identify reserve study problems "by type", provide an example or two of each type — (all our examples are drawn from actual observations) — and add a few words about possible preventive measures you can take. "You", in this case being the receivers of the plans (Board Members, usually), but it would be encouraging to learn that reserve planners themselves are also paying attention!

**Sorry ... Wrong Number**

The essence of a good reserve study lies in the numbers. Two sorts of blunders can render planners' submissions unacceptable. Good old everyday arithmetic accounts for some of them, and these are, frankly, inexcusable. They signal that the specialist hasn't bothered to double-check the figures.

But the other kind is, if anything, even worse. They're errors in formulation and in concept, and they occur because the planner isn't clear on the model or the equation used to arrive at the desired result. Take, for example, the calculation of interest earned on the fund's balances. If you're producing an inflated version of the plan, is inflation applied to the interest amounts? The answer is no; the dollars used as the base on which interest is calculated already have inflation in them. Is interest applied to the annual opening balances, the annual closing balances, or the average of the two? The answer is it doesn't greatly matter, as long as it's consistent. But the latter method is, in our view, preferable. We looked at a plan the other day where the Planner had calculated no interest at all!

Our most vivid interest-related example concerns a plan we saw where grossly overstated interest amounts appeared in the plan. The amounts on that line, in this particular plan, were $240,000 higher, in total, than the figures should have been! Seriously. The plan showed nice positive closing balances over all the years, which made everyone happy. But when we corrected the interest amounts to their proper, lower values, we got negative balances for several years. This necessitated a complete re-work of the whole thing, from square one.

We have yet to determine what "formula" this planner was applying. All we know is … it was as far as you can get from being the right one

How can you ensure your plan is free of these serious defects? There's only one way. Never, never sign-off on a planner's submission report without studying it carefully. Even quick mental arithmetic can catch errors that would otherwise slip by. And if you're unsure how the planner "got" certain figures, make sure he explains it all, with examples.

## Understanding Your Reserve Fund Study

This section is in two parts. One part deals with comprehension — knowing the meaning behind all the numbers, percentages, and ratios ... knowing exactly what messages the study is delivering to you. The other part deals with clarity and "grasp" ... the ability of a good report to deliver its meaning quickly and accurately. Let's start with ...

### Comprehension

True story. An executive of a large mid-western bank was asked by an association to advise it on investing the money in its reserve fund, about $200,000. The banker asked for, and received a copy of the reserve study. His first impression was not good — the whole thing was three pages long, one page of text and two pages of numbers. The common elements were simply listed as "major headings" (grounds, interior, heating air conditioning, etc.) with no detail at all, along with their current replacement costs and the remaining useful life. No spreadsheet, no annual balances, no funding schedule. For this they had paid $3,000! He asked the prospective investors how they used the "reserve study" (intentional quotes), and their answer was, they didn't. They admitted they didn't know how!

There are a couple of issues here. One is that the report was so meager and contained so little information it could be called a travesty of the planner's obligations. Even if the recipients tried to, and knew how to, they would not have been able to derive anything meaningful from this study. It is, admittedly, an extreme case of shoddy work that should not have been accepted. The other issue is that the planner offered no presentation of the report. It was, figuratively speaking, "phoned in".

The above describes an unusually bad scene. But let's, instead, consider a more typical planner's report that includes all the information you'd normally expect to receive — a listing of all the repairable and replaceable components, the expected costs and timing relative to the work required, rates for interest and inflation, a recommended funding schedule both in annual dollars and cost-per-unit terms, and the resulting opening and closing reserve balances. A report like this nicely covers all the bases, but ... do the Board Members really understand it? Actually, many often do not. But they should. Who's responsible, then, for ensuring that everyone "gets it"?

We believe it's a *shared* obligation and that the planner and the Board, both, must ensure that the plan is fully understood.

It's simply essential, that the planner delivers the report personally, and presents it, in person, to the Board. If you're fortunate, the presenter will have the skill to cover the reserve study in the amount of detail that's "just right" — to not skim over it too quickly, and to not dwell unnecessarily on minutiae. He or she will pause frequently to ask if there are questions before moving along to another item. The planner will also emphasize that he or she will be available anytime a Board Member, or the Board as a whole, would like a return visit to clear up any leftover concerns.

By the same token, the Board, in the absence of the planner's offer to present the report, should insist on getting these services. Best idea of all ... build it in to the agreement that's signed when the planner is selected for the job.

## Layout and Display

The other part of "Understanding Your Reserve Study" relates to the "optics" of the report. You may regard this as lightweight stuff, cosmetics, that really aren't all that important. We think they are, and here's why. We all judge everything we see in print as ... (1) easy on the eyes, inviting, a pleasure to pick up, etc., or ... (2) dull-looking, likely to be boring, complicated and dense. If you're like most people you know that what we've just said is true, but you're not sure just why it's true. The fact is, there are lots and lots of great techniques used by skilled report-writers that can increase the comprehension factor enormously, along with the pleasure the reader will get from dealing with it.

We've looked at many associations' reserve studies and found that almost all of them showed room, sometimes lots of room, for improvement. Our most common observation is how depressingly dull a typical black-and-white spreadsheet can be. Hardly anyone can pick one up with the anticipation of having an easy job understanding it.

The figures are often jammed together, and dollars are carried out to the nearest whole dollar instead of being rounded to, say, the nearest "thousand", or if you prefer, the nearest hundred, like $165,678 instead of $166 (the nearest thousand) or $165.7 (the nearest hundred). You'd be surprised how much more inviting the sheet looks when all the unnecessary ink is removed.

One of our gripes is, believe it or not, the "word processing" skills applied to the page. Using bold words or figures where they would help, making the grid lines of a table a light gray instead of black, lining up all the numbers to the right, so you don't have wiggly margins.

And ... what's wrong with using a picture or two? Some bar charts, for example. And if they're in color, even better! There are endless easy opportunities to put life and comprehension into the report.

Moving from style to content, engineers or accountants can readily appreciate the jargon in many reports — accrued this, deferred that, unexpended this, and over-expended that. But terms like those are likely not okay for the ordinary Board Member or Unit Owner who may be a music teacher, or a mechanic or a dentist. RFund software, for example, uses "Money In" and "Money Out". Can't get much simpler than that.

There's something quite wrong when a person must spend several minutes to get "on board" with a report before being able to read it properly. No wonder we feel sorry for non-experts who are most often the recipients of reports like these.

### Insightfulness — and Lack Thereof

We've seen reports where, in places, the planner could simply, well ... have "cared" more. They're not mistakes really, but they indicate that the preparer just didn't go the extra mile that he or she should have.

We're talking about spreadsheets showing a number of consecutive low or almost-nil balances. This is a no-no, and should never have been allowed to find its way to the final report. There are a number of remedies for this situation including building in more funding, changing the timing of some expenditures, and tackling some jobs in stages to spread the costs out. In this latter case, breaking the component data down into sub-components can help a lot.

Another issue arises when a very major job — the roofing restoration comes to mind — is shown in the plan as a 2014 job but doesn't show up again over the duration of the 30-year plan. If your plan is for the 30 years 2011-to-2040, the insightful planner will ask himself when the next roofing job will occur. If the replacement interval is, say, 35 years, the next job will occur in 2049 and will not show up on the plan. Yet, the amount of this expenditure, had the plan had a slightly longer duration, would have probably called for higher contributions beginning well before 2040 to ensure that funding was sufficient by the time 2049 rolled around. An insightful planner would bring this to the Board's attention and recommend that he or she be commissioned to prepare a 40-year plan.

One more. It deals with an incorrect or unlikely sequence of repair operations. We've seen studies where for example, driveway paving work is planned for Year X, and the replacement of water-proofing membranes *below* the driveway is planned for Year X+2. Go figure!

## A Couple of Inconceivables

As with all our examples, these two are also drawn from real observations. They concern the use of the proper opening figures for the plan's spreadsheet. The initial opening balance for any reserve plan must be the real, true, audited dollars in the reserve fund on Day 1 of that year. All too often, however, "some other number" is chosen as the opening balance, effectively rendering all the balances for the subsequent 30 years incorrect! It happens.

Similarly, for the first year of the plan there is a budget, passed and seconded, that lays out the monthly contributions to reserves that will be made. That should be the funding figure used in the first year of the plan. But sometimes it's, once more, "some other number".

## Putting It All To Work

Here's a quick summary of the key points we've made. If you're on the Board make sure you understand the document you get from your planner. Question everything. How the figures were derived, where the estimates came from. Ensure the actual numbers for the first year of your plan are right — if they're not, all the rest of them will be wrong. Ask about the equations used for interest and find out how inflation was applied. In the end, it's your responsibility to see that the plan makes sense.

If you're a planner make sure you triple-check all the mathematics. Once you're satisfied, take it upon yourself to deliver a clear easy-to-understand report.

Lastly, here's a nice surprise offer for you. Send us your plan, in confidence, and we'll take time to study it and return it along with a few objective observations. (No charge, of course). You might be surprised what we come up with!

# Escalating ... Inflating
# They're Not the Same

<u>They may Look the Same. But they're not.</u>
Inflation is something that happens to you. You simply account for its effects. Escalating your owners' contributions dollars is something <u>you</u> do. It's a way of getting sufficient funds into the reserve fund to ensure you'll have adequate balances. This short chapter will explain the differences.

---

Many reserve plans reflect increases in owner contributions, one year to the next. That's often a good thing — not always, but usually. But we frequently encounter signs of confusion regarding the difference between increases based on inflation predictions and increases introduced as escalations. They're not the same thing.

Let's start with annual inflationary increases. It's common practice in reserve plans to show yearly increases due to inflation. These are based on a percentage that is currently in vogue, and this percentage is applied to the owner contribution amounts and to the expenditures estimates. We, ourselves, would be happier seeing reserve plans that were totally presented in today's dollars[1]. But the "tradition" is to show inflated up numbers and there's not much we can do about it. OK, like it or not, we're assuming that your plan will likely show an inflation adjustments over its span.

Almost always, the inflation rate that's applied to each year's figures is the same, year after year, throughout the plan. All

---

[1] Our viewpoint on inflation seems to appear in various places, in a number of contexts in the book. We appreciate your indulgence.

well and good. We can't think of any reason, even from the inflation adherents, to use one inflation rate one year, and a different one the next.

But plans often include, or perhaps should include, another kind of yearly increase. Sometimes the reserve fund balances, when using the same owners' contribution figures year after year (even adjusted for inflation) still result in some end-of-year balances that are too low (risky) or even negative (not acceptable). One way to fix that is to add an extra dollop of contribution dollars to all the years. It's simple, and it'll work. Except that you're quite likely to find that you don't need this added amount in every single year of the plan, but for just in a certain period or a particular time-frame that'll be sufficient to get the balances up to a healthy level.

In other words, you want to escalate the contributions for a 5-year period — (or for 3, or 7, or 11 years .. whatever it takes) — and then go back to your original contributions amount (or level off at the higher, boosted contribution amounts).

Testing various escalation alternatives can be a very good idea. It allows one to fine-tune the contributions so that low, risky balances can be avoided, and at the same time keep the balances from getting unnecessarily fat when they're not required to be.

Using escalations, and *showing them* as escalations removes the confusion that we sometimes encounter when we see increases that aren't clearly interpretable as increases for inflation or increases for escalating. Your plan, in other words, is much more understandable to anyone who examines it.

If you would like an example, with dollar amounts, we would be pleased to send it along to you by e-mail. (The book's format simply doesn't lend itself to this kind of tabular information). Our address is rfund@oliver-group.com.

In summary, escalating is a nifty technique. It can be used on its own, or you can also, separately, include an inflationary component if you want to. Using short-term escalations can elegantly "touch-up" a plan's balances where required, compared with the overkill of crude long-duration, unnecessary, contributions increases.

# Picking Your
# Reserve Planner

The choice of selecting a Reserve Planner is an important one. The Reserve Study that emerges will be the product of the Planner's expertise, experience, methodologies and thoroughness. Rather than ask your candidates whatever "comes to mind", we think this check-list will go a long way towards ensuring that your choice is a good one.

---

## Your Candidate's
## Résumé

Well ... she may not actually have a résumé, as such, but we'll cover the things that would likely be in it if she did. We'll refer to things she'd tell you about her company, and about herself[1]. Later, we'll include items you'd learn from others or things you, yourself, could observe.

## What About His Company

There are pluses and minuses about going with a one-person outfit versus, (at the other extreme), a national multi-branch corporation. Small firms with one, two or three planners are definitely worth looking at. They may provide a more personal touch, they are likely to be conversant with local conditions (building codes, costs), and their qualifications can be every bit as good as planners with big companies.

---

[1] In this chapter we'll use female-gender nouns and adjectives ...she, her, hers, etc. We used the male equivalents in our last edition. It avoids the tiresome "he or she" repetitions which would otherwise be inevitable. It also renders us politically correct.

Larger businesses, however, have more clients (by definition), and if they share their experiences among themselves they may have a greater range of solutions than those with few clients. They may, as well, be able to turn out reports with more "horns-and-whistles" which would add to the overall product. Further, in cases of peak periods, they'd be more able to find a planner to do your work when you wanted it done. The trade-off here is that you might not get the planner you're familiar with to work on your study.

There's no clear-cut answer, but it would be interesting to hear your candidates' answers to this question … "Your company is quite small, (or quite large, as the case may be), compared to others. Can you tell us why you think this would be an advantage for us?"

### Your Candidate, Herself

**Accreditation**. There are a number of accreditations that may be earned by Reserve Planners. The Community Associations Institute in the U.S. offers the designations "RS" (Reserve Specialist) to individuals and "AAMC" (Accredited Association Management Company) to companies that meet certain criteria. In Canada, CCI offers the ACCI (Associate of the Canadian Condominium Institute) designation for those who have completed a prescribed course of study.

States and provinces may mandate the training qualifications and prerequisites required to carry out reserve studies.

Your Reserve Planner should, of course, meet any required standards, but if they are not legally required how important are they? We hesitate to say that no prospect should be considered who cannot show some evidence of having gained accreditation or who does not have a particular certificate, diploma or degree. But having one is without doubt a reflection of the fact that some formal preparation has been undertaken.

**Experience.** You know, experience isn't all it's claimed to be. A clerical worker who stopped learning new things after six months can not be said to have, say, eight years of experience. She's had the same six months of experience sixteen times! "Good" experience would be where the candidate has run into lots of difficult situations, and has found ways to solve them. So instead of asking your candidate to reel off … years in this line of work, numbers of studies, types of properties and so on … ask her to describe two or three thorny situations that required some special thinking. That will tell you a lot more.

**The Client List.** Ask for a list of all her clients he's done reserve studies for during the last six months, or year at the most. Property addresses, contact phone numbers, the works. It's a whole lot better, for obvious reasons, than asking … "Please provide the names and phone numbers of a half-dozen of your recent clients?"

## Your Candidate's
## Positions and Opinions

Different planners approach the task of preparing their studies differently. Board Members may themselves hold views on their own preferred methods. Not only are planners' favored positions worth knowing, but it's also interesting to note whether they recognize that they actually have chosen from available alternatives.

**The question of "cushions"**. It is quite possible to prepare a funding schedule that meets bare minimum requirements. That is, it assumes that all repairs will actually cost the same as they are predicted to cost, and that all repairs will actually be required at the time they are predicted to occur. But we have a very emphatic, standing opinion that in reality, life isn't really that kind to us. To protect your balances from sinking (or disappearing) you need a cushion – extra money in the fund. The cushion is to help take care of the unexpected. Ask the candidate what her position is on how "thick" the cushion should be.

Answers like … "It'll be thick enough to do the job", or … "Our estimates of the cost and timing of future repairs are so accurate you won't need a cushion", are serious downers. You should probably terminate the interview right there and then. It reflects a low or non-existent level of understanding that planning is, well … planning. It's not an exact science, as much as we would like it to be.

The best answer is … "We know that predictions are, by their very nature, subject to error. We'll present a plan to you that has what is, in our opinion, a cushion that could be called "reasonable" to take care of unexpected deviations from pre-dicted costs and intervals. If you'd like to build in a bigger safety net, we can adjust the funding plan, or if you think it's excessive we can reduce it". Hire this candidate!

**Cash Flow Method vs. Full Funding Method**. Ask your candidate which one she uses. If she draws a blank it's not a good sign. She should favor one or the other and be able to explain why. Her actual answer doesn't matter a whole lot — they each have their followers. We favor the Cash Flow Method. The points in favor of one versus the other, by the way, can be found in our chapter "Full Funding or Cash Flow". Please go to page 83.

## How The Candidate Does Her Work
### Physical Inspection

A Reserve Fund Study is most often based on a thorough physical inspection of the property. But not always. In some areas the state or provincial statutes may also mandate periodic, interim reserve updates that are largely financial and are not accompanied by a physical inspection. Staying with this for a moment, our view is that updates of this kind should be done quarterly and our chapter on page 47 will explain why.

Our intent, here, however, is to raise the question of invasive tests. These are tests made to determine the condition of components in cases where it might not be possible, on visual inspection alone, to arrive at a conclusion. Perhaps walls should be opened up, cuts made in the roof, or the use of infrared thermography should be undertaken. Inspections of these kinds obviously carry associated costs. In the planner selection process the possibility of tests like these should be raised and the planner should be asked about the kinds of circumstances she would consider when recommending their use along with the kinds of costs that would be incurred.

Of course, one of the most important factors of all is the necessity of ensuring that all components of the property are included in the study. Our free Components List (see page 128) will help, by the way. Ask your candidate how she ensures no components get overlooked.

### The Planner's Report

We think the words ... report, study and plan, refer pretty much to the same thing. The planner does a "study" of the property. A "report" of the study includes major sections — findings, the overall and specific details of the current condition of the property; recommendations, most of which are reflected in time-lines for repair and replacement, and his plan; schedule — the actual repair and replacement combined with estimated costs along with a contributions program that will provide funding to maintain reserve fund balances that are sufficiently adequate to pay for them. The "plan", then, is this part of the report. It's always in the form of a spreadsheet, or table.

Should the planner simply complete her report, bundle it up, and send it over to the Board? We think not. A "draft" report, in our view, should be prepared first and sufficient copies should be run off for the Board Members to obtain it and examine it. A meeting should be held to discuss the report and to provide an opportunity to improve it. Clarification, for example, would be introduced where it becomes evident it's required.

How about changes to the actual substance of the report. It's impossible to cover all the kinds of possibilities here, but one very important change mustl be noted. The planner will have come up with a recommended funding schedule. It's reasonably common for the Board to want to water it down, particularly if the planner is proposing increases. (And the larger the increases, the higher is the likelihood of the Board's reluctance to accept them). What to do?

Well, the Board's decision is in fact final. But the planner, at the planner-selection stage should let it be known that if the recommended funding amounts in his plan are changed by the Board, there must be a note to that effect in her covering letter which forms part of her Report.

In the planner-selection process the Board might ask the planner if he can work with the Board, should the need arise, to develop alternate funding schedules. They might be called barely adequate, acceptably adequate, and adequate. That way, the Board could explain which funding program they chose, and why.

We have focused so far on the printed word. Reports that are typed-and-bound, so to speak. What about orally presented reports. For the Board they are musts. For the Annual General Meeting they are probably not musts, but they are often welcomed (at least condensed versions are) by the unit owners. The Board should ask the planner candidates whether they would be willing and able to do these and if so, what would the fee be.

Three quick points. Ask the candidate for a <u>sample of her
report.</u> An actual one. Yes, she may have to Find-and-
Replace the real client's *name* with a fictitious one, but you
should see the kind of work she's been turning out. Another
point — you should tell her you'll want your report not only in
traditional bound copies but <u>also as a computer file</u>. No
planner should object to that. Thirdly, you should tell her
you'd expect to see <u>a chart (graph) or two</u> to illustrate his
numbers.

### The Planner's Fees

Her proposed fee, of course, will play an important part in the
selection process. You should tell the candidate that you'd
like her quote to include the entire job … the physical inspection and assessment, the estimates for the timing and costs of
the predicted repairs, and a suggested funding plan to arrive at
future reserve balances. As we suggested earlier in this chapter, you may specify that she deliver a choice of funding plans.
Funding aside, tell her that you'll require that a draft of the
final report should be submitted to the Board and this could
very well necessitate some rewriting before finalization.

She may, in fairness, respond that if re-writing were substan-
tial, or if new requirements, not specified at the outset were
introduced, she may have to charge an hourly or per diem rate
to cover the requested extras.

We believe that quotes from a number candidates are usually
quite alike — they're competitive and it will be reflected, usually, in their fees. We would not necessarily say that those
quoting higher amounts would do superior work. Not at all.

But you may find that the planner you'd most like to engage on the basis of all the other factors happens to be at the higher end of the scale. Then, go with her, even if her quote is higher. At least, tolerably higher. Don't forget that if you're running reserve balances of, say, $500,000 for example, a $2500 premium is not very much (half of one percent) to pay for a study that's done thoroughly and faultlessly.

Finally, we realize that the selection process is time-consuming. That's why we often see it being delegated to Property Managers. But we're not sure many Property Managers go through the kind of selection process we're espousing here. That's why, at the very least, we recommend that the Board itself should be involved with a "short-list" of PM-screened candidates. The Board can make the final choice from the short-list.

### Our Companion Piece

For our views on the shortcomings of some reserve planners — in evidence, happily, in a large *minority* of reserve specialists — turn to page 57 for our chapter Give Me a Break.

Finally, please accept our admission that this chapter was not intended to be exhaustively inclusive. We have covered items that we think are of significant, but they can easily be added to other criteria that you learn elsewhere or, indeed, bring to the interviewing table on your own.

# Reserve Fund Investment Interest

<u>Make Money While You Sleep</u>
Want to have happy unit owners?  Save them some money!
Interest earned on invested reserve fund balances can materially help to keep owners' contributions in check.  This chapter provides workable suggestions to tweak your earnings a bit higher.  It also describes three ways to calculate estimated interest on future planned balances.  One of them is better than the others!

Almost all co-owned properties maintain interest-bearing accounts in which they stash the bulk of the reserve fund balances.  Makes sense of course.  It's an additional source of revenue and helps to mitigate the burden of costs borne by the unit owners.

One idea, if you're not doing it already, is to make sure that you have an absolute *minimum* proportion of your funds residing in non-interest accounts.  With all the banking transactions you can do by computer these days, you should be able to transfer money to-and-from savings and checking accounts to take full advantage of interest payment policies.

Some of the reserve fund money may be in bank deposits that guarantee a higher interest pay-out if you guarantee a specific term (months, years).  They're named differently in the States and in Canada so we're staying away from regional designations.  They pay higher interest rates than savings accounts, but they work only if they're not cashed in earlier than the agreed-upon term. So it'll take a bit of figuring on your part to ascertain when payments for reserve expenditures will likely be made, to ensure that you won't have to cash in these kinds of deposits before their due dates.

One more strategy that can help is to make a deal with your contractor that will enable your property to pay for the work a bit later than you ordinarily would. A typical deal would be to pay each month only for the volume of work actually accomplished. But there are an infinite number of arrangements possible, and sometimes just by indicating that you'd like to stretch the payments out, the contractor will come back with an attractive workable scheme.

Here's another "timing" technique, and it's one that can pay off handsomely if you adopt it. It could literally add hundreds of dollars (maybe more!) to your fund. Simply, try to schedule your reserve fund work, and thus your reserve fund expenditures, late in the year. Your financial year, that is.

Why? Here's what it'll do for you. You have a job that will cost, say, $60,000. If it's done in January, and paid for in February, you'll have that $60,000 in your reserve fund investments for 2 months. You would have earned, for example 4% on it for one-sixth of a year $400. But if it's done in September, and billed in October, you'll earn 4% on it for five-sixths of the year ... $2,000.

Simply by doing the job later, you'll capture an additional $1,600! If you follow that scheme consistently the extra dollars in interest can add up to quite a worthwhile total.

Before we leave this subject, here's an important Alert. Safety is all-important. It comes first. Don't consider deferring work that has a safety-related element. Balcony railings, cracked walkways, certain kinds of electrical work. It's not worth earning extra interest if anyone's safety may be imperiled.

What you can do though, in this case, is get the work done without delaying it but instead, delay paying for it! You can sometimes persuade the contractor to agree to a periodic payment schedule. Maybe. Maybe not. But if you go this route, make sure it's all negotiated before the job begins to avoid being tainted with the reputation for being a poor payment risk.

Let's change gears now and look at how interest calculations can be handled when a reserve fund plan is being created. If you've read our chapter "Reserve Fund Fundamentals — Part Two" you'll be familiar with the next couple of paragraphs. After that, it's new material.

Interest can represent a significant addition to the "money in" element of the plan. So there would have to be a row on your spreadsheet for the interest dollars as "money in". To calculate the interest dollars you'd estimate an interest rate and apply it to the balance in your reserve fund.

But ... which balance — the opening balance for the year? ... the closing balance for the year? ... the average balances for the year? Actually, planners aren't consistent in regard to their choice. We like the last one, the average balance for the year, but the arithmetic is a little harder. Not really hard, but trickier than using the opening balance base (that's the easiest one).

For a software note on this issue, see page 137.

Want to see the arithmetic necessary for these options? We'd be delighted to supply it. It's a bit long for this chapter so what we'll do is send it along by e-mail if you ask us to. Our address is rfund@oliver-group.com

One important area concerning interest on your reserve fund balances is related to where you can get the best return on your money. It's not one that we're going tackle, for a number of reasons. One reason is that the answer varies all the time. Another is your particular view on being locked in to long-term higher-pay-off instruments versus more liquid investments, which don't pay as much. The answer is best found by engaging a reputable financial advisor — (start with your accountant perhaps) — and going into the selection process with him or her.

Our messages in this chapter are ... (1) Interest is an important part of the reserve fund plan ... (2) Earned interest can add significant dollars to your fund ... (3) interest can be calculated, for planning purposes a few different ways ... (4) Get face-to-face, timely advice on your reserve fund investments.

# Full Funding
## OR
# Cash Flow
## LESS IS MORE

<u>Give Me the Simple Life</u>
Here, we make a case, and it's a compelling one, for using one planning method over another. Interestingly the method we espouse is every bit as good (better, we think) and a whole lot easier to produce and understand.

―――――――――――――

One of the things that always gives us pleasure is the discovery of a new way of doing something ... a way that gets the job done just as well, and takes a fraction of the time. Preparing a reserve fund plan can be one of those things. Some planners, perhaps even the majority, use an approach that gets the job done satisfactorily, but takes a whale of a lot of time. Not only is this method time-consuming but the results are loaded with numbers and ratios and percentages that nobody understands and add not a thing to the comprehension of the plan. You've gathered by now, that we don't like it very much. It's called the Full Funding method.

Our much-preferred approach is the Cash Flow method and we're about to explain why it's far and away the better choice.

The starting point is the work that *both* methods employ, at the very start of the planning exercise. They both begin with a component-by-component assessment of each component's metrics. These include the normal useful life of the component, when it was last repaired or replaced, its remaining life, and the cost in today's dollars of repairing it or replacing it. That's a major assignment and it is the very foundation of all reserve fund plans' computations. Once that's done the Full Funding people go one way and the Cash Flow people go another way.

The Full Funding devotees now take these component-by-component data, and using a multi-factor formula which is far from transparent, and quite challenging to explain, (we'll supply it to you if you ask us), derive a funding percentage for each component individually. That is, for each and every component listed for repair or replacement, *a mini-reserve plan is produced* to come up with the funding necessary to ensure that the repair costs for this single component — out of a total of 100 or 200 components — will be adequately funded. When it's done for one of them, they go on to do it for the next one, and the next one and so on. Essentially you end up with 100 or 200 mini reserve plans!

Of course, ultimately all of these numbers are neatly compiled into tables and spreadsheets, but still there are plenty of detailed pages and lots of ink to wade through. The effect of all these percentages, ratios and amounts is that, frankly, they camouflage the plan's overall picture. In the end, the planner says that his recommended plan shows your repairs are 57.4% or 90.3% or 42.0% funded. The Full Funding adherents often state that if you're below 30% funded you risk having insufficient reserves to pay for future repairs but if you're over 70% funded the chance is very unlikely that this will happen. Your authors are bit puzzled by this but assume it's based on experience with various percent funded levels over the years.

Let's turn now to our choice, the Cash Flow method.

To repeat an earlier remark … we start with a component-by-component assessment of each component's metrics. These include the normal useful life of the component, when it was last repaired or replaced, its remaining life, and the cost in today's dollars of repairing it or replacing it today. (Again, these are the same measures as used when doing a plan using the Full Funding strategy). Using these data we prepare a spreadsheet with a title something like "Reserve Plan Expenditures Estimates for 2011 through 2040". The sheet has the components listed down the left-side, and the years across the top. If a particular component needs to be replaced or repaired for $11,000 (in today's dollars) every 8 years and the work was last done in 2008, the amount of $11,000 would be entered in 2016 — (that's 8 years later than the last expenditure), and then entered as well, in 2024, 2032, and 2040.

This routine is repeated for every component so that in the end you have a spreadsheet with repair costs in the years (the columns) that you expect to have to pay them. The spreadsheet, by the way, looks pretty "empty" because most of the cells for given components and years are not filled in with cost dollars.

When all that has been done the columns, one column for each year, are added to arrive at the plan's annual total expenditures. It's the very essence of simplicity, it's understandable, and it makes sense.

Now, the aim of all this is to produce a plan with future balances that are healthy enough to pay for these expected expenditures. Note carefully here, please ... we are not talking about component-by-component balances, we are talking about future *total* balances produced by using the sum total of all expenses.

To obtain healthy balances we must come up with a funding schedule that will tell us how much we need to collect each year from the unit owners to pay for these expenditures. This part is a mixture of science and art, but it essentially means that various funding amounts are "tested" to find out what the balances look like and, in the end, one of the funding attempts (we call them "what-ifs") will emerge as the best one. The best one: Its balances are high enough to cover the cost in every year, and there is a built-in cushion to take care of unexpected occurrences where the expenditures are higher or sooner than predicted[1].

Note that we left the component-by-component detail way back there on the road. We're dealing now only with the *totals*, which is really all that we have to concern ourselves with.

The neat thing about dealing only with the annual totals of the estimated expenditures is that when actual repairs are made the variations from the predicted amounts will, to some ex-

---

[1] To zero in on the level of your required balances and to obtain the adequacy you need to take care of unexpected expenditures you'd use our Adequacy Confidence Ratio and Adequacy Directional Ratio. Please see page 29 for a full explanation.

tent, cancel each other out. Not perfectly, of course, (and sometimes not by a great deal), but they do, at least to some extent, and it makes a great deal more sense to therefore deal with the totals than deal with the numerous elements that make up the totals — the elements will vary quite a bit, individually, from their predicted amounts. The totals won't.

You'll find this interesting. We, for fun, obtained (with permission of course) a number of reserve plans from a very large company in the U.S. who used the Full Funding approach. Yes, heaps of arithmetic and all that. Using only their estimates of *total* annual component expenditures — completely avoiding component-by-component detail — we went the Cash Flow route, using only the annual total expenditures, and worked out contributions schemes that would give the plans their adequate balances. Remember we did not look at funding, component-by-component, as they did. Well, the contributions recommendations were about the same, theirs and ours. We both ended up with good funding schedules and adequate balances but, to arrive at our contributions numbers, we did it with far less arithmetic and spent far less time at it. And ... the resulting information was a great deal more readable and comprehensible.

Yes, you can rely on the Cash Flow method. Here in Ontario, it's *required*, to comply with our Condominium Act. It's used, therefore, for virtually all the co-owned properties in Ontario — all 9,000 of them! It's hard to imagine we'd be sticking with the Cash Flow approach if it wasn't delivering what we needed.

## THE
# Foggy Future

<u>An Often-Overlooked "Given" in Forecasting</u>
There are people who spend their careers in jobs that require them to predict various things. There are plenty of techniques and mathematical models they can use to do their work, many of them highly sophisticated. Luckily, reserve planning doesn't require that kind of expertise, but here's a "notion" that we think you'll find makes sense.

---

It's only a couple of pages. Not too deep, not too complicated. But it came up the other day as we were discussing, by e-mail, a question that was put to us. The question related to the reliability of expenditures forecasts, and our reader asked — "How accurate can we expect these estimates to be?".

It's a good question. But it's not possible to come up with a real number to answer it. Within five percent, fifteen percent? More, perhaps? Who knows. Maybe someday someone (not us though) will do a research study comparing estimates made in Year X with the realties that occurred in Year X+5, X+10, X+30, and so on.

What we'd bet on, however, is that the estimates you make for that deck-painting project that's scheduled 3 years from now is going to be more accurate than your estimate for the same job scheduled for 25 years from now.

So what are the implications of this conclusion for the average reserve fund planner, or Board of Directors? In a word, do the best job you can of estimating your expenditures throughout the range of plan-years, but concern yourselves more, a lot more, with their impact on your balances in the next ten years, than in the final twenty years of your plan.

Keep in mind that you're going to have plenty of time and many opportunities to review and amend your far-out estimates before you even get close to the repair-dates.

One caveat though. If the big, infrequent jobs show the least sign of being seriously higher than reflected in your plan, do, yes DO, make adjustments to your plan at the earliest opportunity. It takes a while to "save-up" in the fund for the big jobs and it's prudent to start saving (i.e., boosting your balances) earlier than later. We've even given this practice a name. We call it "The Watchful Eye Principle". Yes, relax, as you sail along, but keep a watchful eye wide open for shoals and icebergs.

# Your Reserve Fund's Safety Nets

<u>In trouble?</u>  <u>Here's a way out</u>
Can reserve fund balances go wrong?  They certainly can, and
they definitely do!  Your authors explain why reserve funds go
off the rails sometimes.  They also describe three safety nets
that can be deployed for occasions when you need them.  Lifeboats, parachutes, air bags — reserve funds have them too!

When you think about it, we have safety nets everywhere.
Emergency exits on airplanes, lifeboats on liners, fuses in our
electrical systems, etc., etc.  Why?  Because we know that everything doesn't always go as it should.  Airplanes crash-land,
ships hit icebergs, and wires get overloaded.

How about your reserve fund?  You hire a reputable Reserve
Fund Planner.  The Planner inspects the property and comes
up with predictions on when repairs and replacement will be
required, and how much they will cost.  And you set up a
schedule of funding so these things can be paid for when the
time comes.  What can go wrong?

Enter Murphy's famous law … "If something can go wrong,
it will".  Things break down, or wear out, or cease to function,
before they're supposed to.  The cost of replacing or repairing
them is higher than your Specialist expected.  Your healthy-
looking plan suddenly isn't doing the job and you're "in the
red" … or close to it.

Maybe your Specialist wasn't as competent as you thought —
and we quickly add, that's a rarity. But a bit more likely is that
he or she slipped up, when making the plan. Overlooked
something, did some faulty arithmetic. Still not likely but possible. But most likely of all, mechanical or structural parts of
your property simply did not stand up the way they should
have. Kind of "nobody's fault, but it happened".

That's the cost end of things — how about the funding end?
Well, the reserve fund plan included a funding schedule and it
all looked good, at the time. But once in place, after real expenditures began to vary from planned expenditures, nobody
was paying much attention. The predicted balances, had they
been updated with new information would have looked sicker
and sicker, and warning lights would have flashed. With no
warning system in place, your property found itself up to its
neck in quicksand before they realized it.

All right, we've identified three broad areas of cause — the
plan was faulty, the property's components failed unexpectedly early, and the fund balances were not being monitored
properly. Which brings us to …

… our safety net theme. First question: Do you have one?
(A safety net, that is). The answer is "yes", you actually do.
You have three, in fact. Your fund needs an injection of
money, where do you get it? One source — one of your
safety nets — is from a financial institution. The other source
is from your unit owners. And the third source isn't actually a
source at all. It's an "arrangement".

First, the financial institution. We're talking about borrowing. The kind of institution that usually springs to mind is The Bank. And it is, indeed, an option. But you may not know that there are firms that specialize in just the kind of loans we're referring to here. They know all about shortfalls in reserve funds, and they know all about owners' contributions and reserve fund spreadsheets and plans. You'd be surprised if you knew how many properties used their services.

The other source of funds is, of course, the Special Assessment. (We were about to say, "The *dreaded* Special Assessment"). It's safe to say that it's not a good day when the Board announces that all unit owners must write a one-time (hopefully) check for some significant sum. No matter how it's explained a hue and cry is inevitable. It's bad tasting medicine, but if it's swallowed, it works!

Let's compare the Loan with the Special Assessment. The loan will almost certainly call for some increase in monthly fees. It's to abide by the agreed-upon repayment schedule. But the amount, each month, will usually be tolerable because it's spread out over time. Part of the re-payments will be interest on the loan so the amount paid back, in total, will be higher than the actual amount required to fix the fund.

Another thing is that new owners coming in to the property will also be required to pay the higher fees caused by the loan. Higher monthly fees have an affect on resale attractiveness, and that's a consideration.

With a Special Assessment on the other hand it's a "done deal". You get the money that's required, there are no extra costs associated with getting it, the fund is brought back to a healthy position and your crisis is over. On an ethical basis, the people that were there when the fund became ill are the ones that are paying to cure it, not new residents who had nothing to do with the shortfall.

There's no best way. Like many condo issues, some properties will see one alternative as better than another property. Sometimes, even, for good reasons!

All right, we have compared, in some detail the pros and cons of Special Assessments, with Loans. But there is one more lifesaver that could be deployed in some cases. It's called "Financing".

Financing involves entering into a lease-agreement with the supplier. You essentially rent the component instead of buying it. One example would be the chiller unit that's part of your HVAC System. Another would be telecom equipment for switchboards or intercoms.

A question might then arise regarding whether the lease payments would then fall into the operating budget or would be paid for from the reserve fund. And that, dear readers, is something that you'll have to take up with your professionals since it would be subject to an interpretation of your local condominium statutes if any, and your property's bylaws. Tricky, in this regard, but financing is still a good option.

Some infrequent projects, like window replacement for example, can be "financed" by the contractor who performs the work. Suppose you have a $100,000 window job that only takes two months to do. That would ordinarily require two $50,000 payments. Alternatively, financing by the contractor might, instead, require twelve monthly payments of $9,000. The extra $8,000 being the charge by the contractor for floating the cost, and handling the extra paperwork.

Let's end by stressing that the recurring theme of this book is to create a good plan and monitor it continually. Our view is that by doing so you'll come close to eliminating the probability of ever requiring a safety net — a Loan, a Special Assessment, or a Financing or Leasing Arrangement — to save your property from serious financial fiascos.

# Legislation
## Laws & Statutes

### A Brief Coverage of What's Going On
### Along with a Few Opinions

Our book includes lots of ways that persons associated with co-owned communities can run their organizations better. We might even say that, in regard to reserve funds anyway, if our suggested approaches were embraced, there might not be any need at all for protection under The Law. This chapter will look at the legislative picture briefly, and thus add a legal dimension to the other aspects we have covered.

---

Anything "legal" is, almost by definition, long, lengthy and yes, infinitely boring. But if it weren't for laws, where would we be? We might find that if we looked at laws related to causing bodily harm, the prohibitions would be similar across state or provincial boundaries. Same with automobile operation, and with behaving wildly in public. Not so with the operation of co-owned properties.

A quick look at easily accessible sources[1] shows that in the U.S. 36 states have some sort of "Condo" legislation dealing with reserve funds and 14 have none. Of those 36 states that do, many have only minimal legislation. In Canada, 5 provinces have statutes on the books that can be described as "meaningful", and 8 (including Territories) do not.

---

[1] We acknowledge our sources as (1) In the U.S, the book "Reserve Funds: How and Why Community Associations Invest Assets" (2005), and (2) In Canada, the book "Reserve Funding for Condominiums" (2003).

We feel it's likely that at least some of our readers have some sort of interest in actively engaging themselves in efforts to improve existing laws in their areas, or if they have no legislation at all, to persuade their governments that statutes should be drawn up.

To that end, we'd simply like to bring to your attention, Ontario's "Condominium Act, 1998". Ontario is Canada's most populous province, with an estimated 7,500 condominium corporations (and hundreds more, it seems, being built each year). Your authors are familiar with the Condo Act (its short name), and we thought it worthwhile to bring it to your attention — parts of it, at least, could perhaps serve as models for similar statutes in your region.

To see the Act in its entirety you can go to the website of the CCI, the Canadian Condominium Institute. CCI is the Canadian equivalent of the CAI in the states — the Community Associations Institute. It's at

ccitoronto.org/Condoact/default.asp.

We think the Condo Act is possibly one of the better statutes around. Seems to cover all the bases, and covers each one in detail.

The reserve fund section is Section 93. In connection with reserve funds, we believe, again, that the coverage is protective, as it should be, but we'll just take a minute here to mention three issues that could use some attention, in our opinions.

These three issues are …

- The absence of any requirement to submit information to a government branch to ensure that the Boards are acting in compliance with the Act. For example, the Act requires that certain financial tables be prepared related to the reserve funds of the corporations, but beyond the requirement to distribute them to the unit owners, there is no central "check" on their completion or soundness.

- The word "adequate" is used to describe the proper level of reserve fund balances, but there is no definition of adequacy. Our approach to the matter, covered in this book, is one that may be considered — an objective, well-defined, quantitative definition of what an adequate balance really looks like. There are no doubt other approaches as well, but so far they seem not to have emerged.

- A "grey area" that needs some attention, is the difference between maintenance and operating expenses. Some maintenance costs clearly end up as reserve fund expenditures, and properly so. Periodic overhaul of elevators would be an example. But others are more nebulous. Doing pointing work on brick facings for instance.

Obviously, legislation is a mammoth area to tackle, and we have had to limit our treatment of it to the material you've seen, above. In any case, in the right hands at the right time, we trust some of you will find it of value.

# What's Wrong
## with a
# Special Assessment Anyway?

<u>We Examine the Aversion to Special Assessments</u>
If you're like most unit owners, getting a special assessment notice does not make your day. It most often is an unexpected bill, and therefore it's an outlay that may be difficult to pay. It also signals that perhaps "somebody hasn't done his job" and that's also not comforting. This chapter takes a look at the different sides of the question — there's always more than one, you know.

---

It seems to us that people these days have a natural tendency to be divided in to "camps". Controversy is more widespread than ever — you only have to look at the political news to get lots of examples. If there are those that believe "this" is the way to go, then others are sure "that" is the way to go.

Why should reserve fund issues be different. No surprise — they aren't! One camp, we'll call it the "risk averse"[1] camp likes to see a nice comfy reserve fund that includes a thick cushion. That means that the fund balances are high enough to withstand cost eventualities that could *possibly* occur, but probably will not. The chances are, with a fund like that, the day will never come when the fund runs dry because of unpredicted (or poorly predicted) costs.

---

[1] This notion is tackled in our chapter on the adequacy of reserve fund balances, as well.

The other camp is the "risk prone" group. These owners will say "Predicting the future accurately just isn't possible, so there's no point in putting away extra money to cushion predictions that will turn out to be inaccurate anyway". They are quite ready to accept that in some future years the reserve fund will, in fact run dry. Expenditures will, indeed, be required to pay for repairs that come in at higher-than-predicted levels, or that come in earlier than expected, or that were not predicted at all. In actual fact, it would be rare to find camps that were, as the saying goes "miles apart". But it's not rare to find camps, say at your Annual General Meeting, who favour a safe fund with "some" cushioning in there, versus those that tend to be on the pay-as-we-go side.

Some of the arguments used by the "risk prone" camp would include:

- I want my money in my pocket instead of in the reserve fund. If the property needs money I'll pay for it when it's needed.

- I may not live here forever, and perhaps I won't benefit at all from the money I've paid into the reserve fund to make it extra safe for possible future exigencies. It will benefit someone else, but not me.

- I'm at a stage in my career where I expect my earnings to grow, and I'll be in a better position to pay higher fees in the coming years.

We must say, statements like that are not at all unreasonable. But neither are the assertions of those who would prefer to pay a level of fees high enough to reduce the possibility of running into a special assessment.

All this brings us back to the title of this chapter — So what's wrong with a special assessment anyway?

For one thing, (a strictly human nature oriented answer), the announcement of a special assessment always results in owner unhappiness. The Board gets blamed for not running the property suitably. The question is asked (and it's often asked by persons who would be among those against higher, cushion-providing monthly fees) why did the Board "let" the balances get so low? Sometimes the reserve plans that were approved by successive Boards were *knowingly* risky, but the former Boards found it easier to propose, and get, approval, for plans that called for low fees rather than high fees. They chose the easy way. No fuss, no muss. But it's the current Board that bears the brunt of the criticism.

Okay, that's the political take on it. But what about the hard-nosed dollars-and-cents part? A certain proportion of the owners will promptly pay up and look forward, not back. But others will delay, and they'll introduce collections problems. Perhaps some will not pay at all and there will be threatened or actual foreclosures. Word will get out to the marketplace and the value of the units will drop. Selling your unit and moving out will become an even more disagreeable decision than it normally is. And yes, even the owner with all the "not unreasonable" arguments we listed earlier, will be affected, to a lesser or greater degree.

There's also the house-of-cards effect where one problem begets another. To explain, you have a special assessment. It's not popular, to say the least. But the special assessment is designed to take care of only the pickle you're currently in. The chances are that even when the emergency has been taken care of, you'll need to raise the contributions to the fund to ensure that you'll not need another one. Unpopularity doesn't begin to express it! Resistance will be high and the owners will veto the higher fees, which means ... needed repairs won't get done, the infrastructure will deteriorate, the community will get shabbier and ... well, must we go on?

Our position must be obvious to you by now. We're solidly in favour of planning for future reserves balances that will cover all the "known" future expenditures as well as the inevitable unexpected expenditures. The message: You need a thick-enough cushion built into your future balances to act as a defence against the need for assessments.

Finally — true to our chapter title, we've stuck, so far, to considering the pros and cons of special assessments. But what about other bail-out manoeuvres? For these, please see our chapter on "Safety Nets". It covers a few points regarding assessments, but also tackles the issues of obtaining loans, or arranging for financing your expenditures when necessary. Interesting stuff!

# Your Reserve Fund's Shock-Absorbers

Your Fund's Pain-Killers

Almost everyone knows that reserve funds are created to protect unit owners from"something". But from what, exactly? We think it boils down to three risks, essentially. And they are risks that are well-worth avoiding.

Most of the time we think of a reserve fund as a cache of money to be used, when required, to handle major repairs and replacements. Not a bad description really, but perhaps it would be more accurate to see it more as three caches of money that are in place for three eventualities.

Some people call them *cushions*. We'll call them three "shock-absorbers".

## Bumpy Roads

The first one — and it's one that almost everyone would think of right away — is a shock-absorber to even out the "bumps in the road" when the big bills come in. A good reserve fund plan shows relatively smooth owners' contributions, even though the expenditures from the fund are bumpy — more volatile. Thus, by planning carefully, a few years of high costs would not result in high fees, because the high costs were anticipated. They were "saved for" earlier so they wouldn't be unduly burdensome when they occurred.

That's the shock-absorber effect at work in a well-managed fund. It's sensible, and it works.

But there are two more shock-absorbers that should be in your plan.

### Deviations from Forecasts

One of these addresses the problem of expenditures almost never being quite what they were expected to be. Even the most experienced and professional Reserve Fund Specialist would admit that histories of actual payouts versus the costs that were forecast will show that expected-to-actual variances, some small, some not-so-small, are normal, throughout any period you chose to examine.

We all know why. Costs come in at levels that simply were not the levels you expected. More work was necessary to do a job than the planner predicted. Happens all the time. Or repairs planned for 2015 became necessary in 2012.

Doesn't mean the plan was "no good". It's a fact of life that forecasts are always wrong. Luckily, most of the time they're wrong by tolerable differences, (and sometimes they're not), but they're wrong just the same. Hence the need for Buffer Number Two — another shock-absorber.

What this means in practice is that you should not plan your reserve fund balances "too close to the line". In other words, if you could rely 100% on the fact that all the estimates of costs — their level, and their timing — were correct, you could literally run your balances in some years at close to zero.

You'd "know" that going over estimate was not going to happen, so you'd "know" you'd be safe from going in the hole.

But in reality you cannot know this, so you have a shock-absorber to, essentially, take care of the forecast-to-actual variances that are sure to occur.

### Being Blind-sided

Now for your third and final shock-absorber. It's a bit like the last one, but, if anything, bigger. It's the shock absorber you need to handle occurrences that are totally unexpected. And there are two types of these. One of them can be called "natural" occurrences ... of the unexpected kind. The other kind stems from legislative changes that are imposed by outside bodies.

Natural occurrences are, if anything even more unexpected even than the unexpected variances discussed initially. At least with the variances, you did expect a repair cost, it's just that the amount of it and the timing of it was off. In this case, however, you are blind-sided by a driveway that caved in due to an underground stream you didn't know was there or the discovery that inferior metal was used in the stress rods for the garage floor and they have all rusted. Or that winds reached a velocity never before experienced in your area and badly damaged the roof.

Legislative effects — these can be really costly. Let's look at some possibilities.

- Fire Code retrofit requirements to bring building components to current flame spread and fire separation ratings.

- Elevating devices by-laws demanding that one elevator be equipped with special firefighter over-rides.
- Pending Environmental legislation requiring that only R-123 refrigerants be used.
- Playground equipment safety legislation.
- City bylaws requiring particular underground garage painting and signage standards.
- Building Code changes restricting the height and configuration requirements of balcony and stair guards.

We're going to insert an anecdote here, stemming from the fire regulations item, above.

---

A particular community experienced a fire in a high-rise where the damage from smoke and heat was considerable. No one was hurt, but it was a wake-up call to explore ways of lessening the potential risk in any future events.

One of the recommendations was to require, for all similar buildings in the city, better hallway doors for each unit. The recommendation became law, and an expensive project was undertaken to replace all the doors in these buildings. The Boards, of course, complied with the new law — they installed the new, more costly doors and used their reserve funds to pay for them. These expenditures were unexpected, and properties that had marginal slack in their funds had to find ways to bring their reserves back up to scratch.

So far, our story could be described, as "thought-provoking". But it gets worse. The new doors, as it turned out, besides providing added protection, were also quite soundproof, rendering the hallway-situated fire bells ineffective. This meant installing alarms inside each unit, which greatly added to the cost of the project. An unexpected increase to an already unexpected requirement.

An added complexity is the question of the payment for the bells. Since they are inside the premises of each unit, would they be a reserve expenditure — they were after all necessitated by the doors — or should they be billed to the owners, individually?

The matter of defining what is, and what is not, a reserve expenditure is still another reason for building in some shock absorption!

---

Getting back to our thread, that's the lot! We've discussed a number of situations that all have one thing in common. Namely ... they all make even the best-laid plans go askew. Nothing is certain, except of course uncertainty itself. Hence the need for protection.

Yes, we know, you can't just have a couple of hundred thousand dollars lying around just in case of a highly improbable contingency. But these kind of events usually call for at least some emergency work and a few thousand dollars would be just the ticket to get it done fast, before a loan or special assessment or even an insurance payment were arranged for.

Our lessons for today. Don't rely, more than you should, on the exactness of your expenditure predictions. Don't plan for a reserve fund that runs its balances too close to the line. Don't dismiss the idea of having a little extra put away for the true emergency situation, should it ever arise.

There's a related question, of course. It's ... given the principles above, how do we calculate the right amounts to keep our reserve funds consistently healthy? We've tackled that in the chapter called ... "Reserve Fund Balances — What Does 'Adequate' Mean?" It begins on page 29. Take a look at it. We're sure you'll enjoy it as much as this one!

# Your Reserve Fund Plan Inflation: Forget About it?

<u>A Reserve Fund Dilemma</u>
The usefulness of showing inflated dollar-amounts in a reserve fund plan is arguable.  In this case we make a strong case for creating the plan using only "today's" dollars (uninflated), and suggest that producing a plan that displays inflated values has little merit — except that people will ask for it if you don't! Read this chapter and see if you agree.

---

Forget about inflation?  Our answer is essentially ... yes.  The importance of inflation in reserve fund planning is highly overrated.

This opinion, we know, is not universal.  Far from it.  We're told that it's essential to account for the effects of inflation when preparing a reserve fund plan.

But we believe there are several things wrong with introducing inflation into your plan.  Please stay with us as we explain what they are.

One of them is — you've got to create your expenditures plan and your funding schedule in today's dollars anyway.  So what's the point of inflating them when you've done all the real work without the inflation factor?  Well, there is one, but it's not terribly convincing.  It's simply this: The point of inflating your basic uninflated dollars is that "traditionally", people like to see them ... the inflated numbers.  Why?  We're not sure, but traditions die hard, and this one's been around for a while.

The point is, your future expenditures are planned for by using the costs, today, of doing the repair work. Decisions must be made regarding how often every given repair should be done, and whether the work should be done in stages. And so on. Then the figures, in today's dollars are plugged in. That's how the expenditures plan is created.

For your owners' contributions, decisions are made in regard to whether or not the expenditures (in today's dollars) call for a funding level of "x" dollars a year, or "y" dollars a year, and whether they should be level throughout the plan period, or whether they should show a decreasing trend, or an increasing trend. Or a little of each. And all this work is done in today's dollars, as well.

Once these decisions are made, there you have it. You're done.

Well, maybe you're not. Because, as we remarked earlier, there are people who'll insist on wanting to see all those numbers, "after inflation". All well and good, but what inflation rate do you use? If you asked a dozen friends (or residents, or reserve fund specialists) they'd give you a dozen answers, all different. Which answer will be closest to reality?

We'd also contend that the inflationary effect on condo expenditures would rarely resemble the inflation estimates for the economy as a whole or for consumer prices if you were inclined to use those indices as a base. Why? Because the things that a condo spends money on ... utilities, wages, the hourly rates for elevator repairers, the price of oil-based tar for the driveway, don't behave like the general indices do.

So not only are inflation rate choices inherently problematic, but estimating them for condo work is even trickier.

Having said all that, people will want to see inflated numbers, so, okay, pick a number and stick it in there. For one thing, they will show that owners' contributions will be raised a little bit each year because of inflation, and that may provide the traditionalists with the numbers they like. Otherwise it's quite ineffectual. But we have to concede that the delivery of a reserve fund plan without them wouldn't be accepted. That's why reserve fund software[1] allows for the display of both the uninflated values and the inflated values despite our feeling that the latter doesn't really add anything useful to the output.

Finally, we're aware that other viewpoints and arguments exist. If you'd like to offer yours, please feel very welcome to get in touch with us.

And ... (finally, finally) ... we suggest you refer to our chapter "Escalating, Inflating. They're Not the Same" that begins on page 67.

---

[1] Please see our chapter on reserve fund software that begins on page 137.

# Reserve Fund
# Expenditures
# Are Not Isolated Events

<u>Bring Today's Experience to Tomorrow's Planning</u>
Most isolated events have few consequences, beyond the event itself. But expenditures from a reserve fund often do. They clearly signal that changes to the existing plan should be considered in light of current expenditure experience. This chapter explains why, and suggests exactly what you should do about them, with a view to keeping your reserve fund balances healthy.

---

If you're into reserve funds ... as a Board Member, a Property Manager[1], a Reserve Fund Specialist, an Accountant ... we hope you won't be surprised to learn that a single expenditure has far-reaching consequences.

Let us explain.

Here's a simple case related to replacing your condo's hallway carpeting. The plan called for its replacement in 2014, but because of its condition you did the job in 2012. The cost, $45,000, found its way into your books of course. But the estimated cost ($35,000) still sits in your reserve fund plan, in the 2014 column.

---

[1] The function called "Property Manager" is also called "Community Manager" or "Association Manager". It seems to be related to the state or province you happen to be in.

Anyone referring to the 2014 plan, unless they're extra careful, is going to see that cost as "coming up" instead of "taken care of".

We maintain that you should do something to head off wrong interpretations. And we have a suggestion for what you should do. We'll get to that a bit later.

But let's go on a bit with other meaningful chain effects that our carpeting replacement is causing.

For one thing, the carpets cost $10,000 more than you expected them to. If, in your reserve fund plan, you have carpet replacement costs in there every 8 years, perhaps all those estimates are low as well. The chances are very good they are, because your planner was thinking $35,000, not $45,000.

(By the way, we're putting aside the inflationary calculation in this chapter. The principles are the same, regardless).

So here you are with a plan that shows a replacement cost of $35,000 several times (every 8 months) in the carpeting row of the spreadsheet, when it should be showing $45,000. Imagine what that variance is doing to your projected balances. It's showing them artificially too high because the expenditures are artificially too low. And the error is increasing as you go through the plan's span.

There's more.

Remember, in our example, that the carpet was replaced 2 years sooner than the plan called for. The plan called for an eight-year interval and you replaced it after only six years.

Your plan, however, is showing a carpet replacement cost occurring every eight years. That interval is now suspect, and you should consider changing it to 6 years for the remaining years of your plan.. What a difference it will make to your projected balances a few years out!

Our point is that a single expenditure from the fund can, and does, have broad, costly, and compounding implications.

All right, how do you handle this? In a word, you adjust your plan as real expenditures occur. You adjust it not only for the single actual expenditure dollars being different than the estimate, but you adjust it also for the probability that later, similar expenditures will resemble the latest expenditure and not the earlier planned amounts. You also adjust your plan for the change in intervals if you think the interval in the plan now looks too long, given your latest experience.

In this short chapter, we cannot go into the how-to's of making these adjustments, but if you go to our website at oliver-group.com/rfund you'll find our Decision Expediter offered for free under "More Free Things". We're sure you'll find it helpful.

Our message, summarized ... you'll rest easier if you're "on top" of your property's reserve fund.

## FOR OPERATING BUDGETS
# Preparing
YOUR
# One-Year Operating Budget

<u>A Mini-Manual for this Important Annual Exercise</u>
To our mind, preparing your annual operating budget is a lot less complex than producing an every five or six-year reserve fund plan. But, like every property-related responsibility, it's got to be handled right. This chapter will help.

---

It's not a difficult job. (Do we hear a sigh of relief?). But it's a once-a-year job, and it often involves people who are new to the property's Board. Some of these people are, as well, not inclined by nature to be skilled budget preparers. This short document is intended to cover the basics related to the preparation of a property's operating budget. Please note that the topic does <u>not</u> relate at all to the task of creating a *reserve fund plan*. That's the *other* dollars-associated exercise that all communities must tackle. Reserve fund plans happen to be our principal pre-occupation, but for this paper we focus only on the Annual Budget.

Here's a step-by-step process for coming up with an annual budget that will nicely see you through the coming year. This is also a good place to tell you that Graham Oliver's company, Oliver Interactive, Inc. also has a new software product called The Budget Machine that'll take the work out of budget preparation, and do a lot more as well. Full details follow our general material on budget preparation.

## SECTION ONE
# Budget Preparation

### Look at Your History

Use your real expenditures over the last couple of years to arrive at your new figures. If gardening costs were $15,000 two years ago and $17,000 last year, use at least $17,000 if you have no new information to the contrary.

### Acquire New Information

A call to your gardening company will tell you what their thinking is for the year ahead. Even better, this might be the time to get some new quotes — from competing gardening companies and other service providers — to ensure you're getting decent prices.

### Look Ahead

Don't assume that the forthcoming year will be a carbon copy of the year just ending. Think about possible changes to your current operating practices or to your existing community environment. If (gardening again) you're considering putting in some new flower beds at the community's entrance-way, build those changes into the budget. If you feel it's time the superintendant got a raise, build that into the budget.

### Synchronize expense estimate with payment-times

When you slot the estimated expenditures into the monthly columns make sure they're put into the months the particular bill is paid. If your annual insurance premium is $12,000 payable in quarterly installment, put $3,000 into each of Feb, May, Aug and Nov. That way your actual outgo will be in sync with your budget.

## Calculate Your Monthly Unit-owner Fees

Arrive at your monthly "Money In" needs. Ordinarily they'd be, entirely, fees collected from the unit owners. But some communities manage to earn a bit of interest on their unexpended balances as well. To earn interest you'd need an interest-bearing bank account in addition to your checking account. And you'd need to pay attention, actively, to these accounts to work out timely and prudent transfers between them.

Your monthly owner-fees collections that are intended for operations (that is, *not* intended for the reserve fund) should be *the same* each month. No owner wants his or her monthly payments to be for different amounts. Coming up with a good monthly amount is dependant on four things. (1) Your opening balance for the budget year. (2) The expenditures you anticipate. (3) The degree of safety you think will ensure always-positive balances even in spite of unusual occurrences. (4) The pattern of your anticipated expenditures.

Your year's Opening Balance for the operating end of your banking will probably be an *estimated* amount as the current year has almost certainly not ended. It's a very important figure however. Try to forecast it as accurately as possible,

Your anticipated monthly total expenditures are entered on the grid. Just the totals, month-by-month. This might be a good time to also suggest that in settling on your numbers for anticipated expenditures, if you were choosing between estimates on the high side versus the low side, you should choose the higher amounts. This will automatically skew your resulting cash requirements upward, which is a good conservative thing to do.

For a quick and effective way to set your fees, turn to our "Sensible Fee-Level" chapter. It provides a routine that'll do the job. Or ... take a look at our software, The Budget Machine, if you want to save doing the arithmetic yourself.

Our approach to fee-setting — whether you do it manually or by using our software — will let you ensure you don't have any months with negative balances in your budget. As well, you can choose the degree of "cushion" you're most comfortable with. You can choose if you'd like to operate close to the line or if you'd like to have some room to maneuver when unexpected costs arise.

The above is "it". Not really difficult at all but approached in a way that's logical and intended to arrive at good, safe numbers. The final layout of the budget would be a table (spreadsheet) that lists the months across the top, with rows down the side for the expense items. If you have a number of expense items you will want to group them into categories — Wages and Salaries for example might include separate items (One item per row) for the payments to the Property Manager, the superintendant, the pool lifeguard, and the cleaning staff.

## Wrapping Up

The material above, we feel, delivers most of the processes you'll need to produce a good solid budget. You can do the whole thing using a pencil and paper (not recommended), or using your computer along with Excel (a bit better) or trying our product The Budget Machine (dare we say, "best"). Please see our chapter on it in this book to learn more about it.

## SECTION TWO
## The Budget Machine

The Oliver half of your writing team of Juffs & Oliver has developed a nifty software product called, simply "The Budget Machine". Here's what it's all about.

### The Inputs

The BMachine (for short) has its inputs and outputs, as most software does. The inputs are …

(1)  The monthly estimates of expenses for all the items that the operating budget is designed to handle, and

(2)  The fees that must be collected, monthly, from the owners to pay for these anticipated expenses.

Of course, the fees collected for keeping the reserves healthy are tacked on to the operating budget fees to arrive at the total monthly payments the owners must make.

The BMachine has a remarkable "accordion" style **built-in spreadsheet** that allows the user[1] to enter the expense estimates for each Item. The Items can be grouped under Categories. For example you may have a Category called Landscaping, and under it are a few Items such as Driveway, Pool, Clubhouse, Tree maintenance, and so on. The accordion means you can run "tight" to look at just the Category figures

---

[1] that would be the Board, the Property Manager and/or your accountant.

or you can "expand" to open up any or all Categories to see the Items in them. Very neat indeed.

The other input is handled by the Budget Machine's **Fee-Setter.**

The Fee-Setter allows you to choose a fee-level that will be fair to your unit owners and provide you with safe working balances at the same time. The fee-levels produced by the process explained below do not include any provision for contributions to the reserve fund. Reserves contributions would be tacked on to the decided-upon fees for the operating expenditures.

Our Budget Machine software includes this Fee-Setter approach as one of its features. This write-up is for users of The Budget Machine as well as for others who might wish to simply use the model we've developed to work out their optimal fee without the help of The Budget Machine.

The Fee-Setter's basic principle is that the monthly amounts from the fees paid into the property by the unit owners should be —

- The same amount each month in any 12-month period
- Should result in the property's bank balances never going below zero — that is, they should never *plan* to go below zero
- And ... the balances should somehow be related to the average monthly planned expenditures.

Let's say, for example, that your property's annual operating expenditures are $240,000. Well you might say then that the average monthly expenditure would be $20,000. Therefore, you might say, that you should set the fees at $20,000/mionth.

Makes sense. Yes? The answer: No, it does not!

For one thing your planned expenditures are not the same each month. Sometimes they're high sometimes they're low, and the funny thing is most of the high months seems to come during a certain short period and most of the low planned expenditures seem to come during another short period. The "pattern" can affect the money you need to collect each month.

Look at these examples. (All numbers in thousands). Example One has fees coming in at a steady $40/month. ($40,000/month). And it has an expenditures pattern that is high in the first six months (60, 50 every month), and lower in the last six months (40, 30 every month). The overall average expenditures/month is 45/month. But the point to focus on is that in a couple of months in mid-year the balances get to perilously low levels. Levels that, if there were some items coming in over budget, the property's balances would go negative.

**EXAMPLE ONE**

|    | J | F | M | A | M | J | J | A | S | O | N | D |
|----|-----|-----|-----|-----|-----|-----|-----|-----|-----|-----|-----|-----|
| OB | 100 | 80 | 70 | 50 | 40 | 20 | 10 | 10 | 20 | 20 | 30 | 30 |
| IN | 40 | 40 | 40 | 40 | 40 | 40 | 40 | 40 | 40 | 40 | 40 | 40 |
| EX | 60 | 50 | 60 | 50 | 60 | 50 | 40 | 30 | 40 | 30 | 40 | 30 |
| CB | 80 | 70 | 50 | 40 | 20 | 10 | 10 | 20 | 20 | 30 | 30 | 40 |

Example Two has fees coming in at a steady 40/month —
same as Example One. But it has an expenditures pattern that
is low in the first six months (40, 30 every month), and higher
in the last six months (60, 50 every month). The overall average expenditures/month over the whole year is still
45/month. But the point to focus on is that the balances
never get into the danger zone.

**EXAMPLE TWO**

|    | J | F | M | A | M | J | J | A | S | O | N | D |
|----|---|---|---|---|---|---|---|---|---|---|---|---|
| OB | 100 | 100 | 110 | 110 | 120 | 120 | 130 | 110 | 100 | 80 | 70 | 50 |
| IN | 40 | 40 | 40 | 40 | 40 | 40 | 40 | 40 | 40 | 40 | 40 | 40 |
| EX | 40 | 30 | 40 | 30 | 40 | 30 | 60 | 50 | 60 | 50 | 60 | 50 |
| CB | 100 | 110 | 110 | 120 | 120 | 130 | 110 | 100 | 80 | 70 | 50 | 40 |

One other thing worth noticing is that the fees, being set at
40/month, produce a closing balance for the year (40) that is
quite a bit lower than the year's opening balance (100). It
would be up the Board to say whether they thought the plan
for a lower year-end balance was all right, or not. If not the
fees could be raised to 45/month which would bring the year-
end balances (in both examples) up to 100, which is the same
as the year's opening balances.

Our Fee-Setter looks primarily at the lowest monthly balance
(singular) when a given fee-level is considered, and compares
it with the plan's average monthly expenditure. It says, first of
all, that if there's a monthly balance under "0" you have to
increase the fees to ensure there are no negative balances. It
*then* says that if your new trial monthly fee-level shows that
the month with the lowest balance has a balance that is between zero and 25% of the year's average monthly expenditures figure — in our examples above the monthly average
expenditures are 45 — that would be a Barely Adequate plan.

Example One with two low month's of 10, would be a Barely Adequate plan because the balance of 10 is only 22% of the average monthly expenditures figure.

All the ranges look like this.

- **Below 0.0**                  **Unacceptable**
- **Above 0.0 to under .25**    **Barely Adequate**
- **Above .25 to under .50**    **Tolerable**
- **Above .50 to under .75**    **Reasonable**
- **Above .75 to under 1.0**    **Well-Cushioned**
- **Above 1.0**                     **Bullet-Proof**

Going back to Example Two, where the lowest month's balance is 40 and the average monthly expenditure is 45 the plan would be in the Well-Cushioned range. They could decide to lower the fee by one or two thousand dollars but it would not have much impact on the owners' payments and it would leave December in a risky situation.

There you have it. The actual method used by the Fee-Setter in our product, The Budget Machine. The above allows you to arrive at the best fee-levels manually, and it's not difficult. If you use the Budget Machine to do it, it will let you carry out what-ifs in a bang-bang fashion so you get to your answer a lot easier and a lot faster.

All of the just-described BMachine inputting features refer to the task of creating your Operating Budget. There's inputting as well that occurs as you track your expenses as you move through the year. That's when, monthly, you input the actual expenses for each item so that you can get comparisons between your planned numbers (your budget, actually) and your actual performance. Once you've gathered your monthly actuals together, you can input the dollar amounts into the BMachine in less than 10 minutes.

## The Outputs

The BMachine provides some great outputs which give you the **information** you need to keep on top of your operations every single month. Not only "just" keep on top of them, but get an actual computer-generated analysis showing variances between actuals and budget — for each and every item large-and-small if you like, or just the key items in each category. And how about seeing a prediction, every month, of how the year will end on a budget-compared-to-actuals basis? The BMachine will do that too!

All of this information is displayed by the BMachine in exceptionally easy-to-read and attractive graphics that even the most numbers-challenged reader can instantly understand. All the heavy-lifting has been done by the BMachine. We've included a whole raft of ingenious Property Management Tools as well. Like an Arrears Log that records the status, and the history, of outstanding fee-collections ... Property Facts folder to keep all your pertinent info like Board member and staff records ... Everyday Notes with special Find and Look-up features.

The BMachine will be ready during the early part of 2011. Please send us an e-mail at rfund@oliver-group.com to order your copy. If you tell us you're a reader of this book, we'll provide you with a nice discount.. You'll love The Budget Machine.

## FOR OPERATING BUDGETS
# The Relationship
### OF
# Operating Budgets
### TO
# Reserve Fund Contributions

<u>The Two Main Parts of Every Property's Financial Control</u>
This chapter will put to rest, once and for all, we hope, the notion that your reserve fund should bear some relationship to your operating costs. We see it everywhere, we'd feel a lot better if we didn't. For your sake, not ours, actually.

---

We could make this the shortest chapter in history by simply saying ... there isn't one! That's right, there is no real relationship[1] between the operating budget of a co-owned property and its reserves funding — whether it be an apartment, a townhouse, or a gated homeowner's association. If your monthly operating costs go up or down they do not cause expenditures for major repairs to change. If major repairs go up or down (they're the repairs that are paid for from your reserve fund), they do not cause any change to the operating expenses.

This example will show why.

We have Condo A and Condo B. Both are about the same size. Condo A has operating costs that include 24-hour front-desk security seven days a week. Also, Condo A was designed poorly, at least in respect to its heating, ventilation and air-conditioning. Heat escapes in winter through single-pane

---

[1] Usually called a "causal" relationship, where a change in one variable causes a change in the other.

windows. Heat comes in during the summer due to big expanses of glass facing south. Condo A has an oil-burning heating system. These and other things contribute to high operating costs.

Condo B has a one-shift per week-day security person. Its architect was energy-savvy and took pains to design this structure in an energy-efficient manner. The fuel used in Condo B is natural gas but it is supplemented by solar panels on the roof.

Both buildings however have about the same contributions requirements for their reserve funds. Say, $40,000/yr. But Condo A has an operating budget of $400,000/yr and Condo B, an operating budget of $200,000/yr. For Condo A, the contribution to reserves would be equal to 10% of its operating budget and for Condo B it would equal 20%. So, if the "rule" were 10%, Condo A would be funding properly and Condo B would be underfunding, by half. Using a percentage of your operating budget to arrive at your reserves contributions, therefore, is a very poor idea,

Do bus driver's salaries have a relationship to the price of Lexus cars? Yes, I guess they do. Bus drivers require pay hikes over time. Lexus prices will increase over time. But to suggest that bus drivers' wages should be tied to the price of Lexus automobiles would be daft, to put it mildly. There's no "real" relationship between them. To end this part on a light note, it was found, we kid you not, that there is a very close correlation between the salaries of school teachers in Minnesota and the price of rum in Havana. Not one of us, we're sure would argue that one causes the other!

Funding for reserves should be determined by a thorough line-by-line study of anticipated repairs and replacements. And the fee-level for operating expenses should be based on a line-by-line exercise of recent and current costs for your particular property. An over-simplified rule-of-thumb like a percentage of the operating budget may be easy to understand, but it doesn't make sense.

### Predicting Operating Costs and Reserve Fund Expenditures

It's useful, we believe, to examine the differences between the two kinds of Money Out. One kind, *anticipated operating costs*, end up as an Operating Budget. The other kind, *estimated expenditures from the reserve fund*, end up as part of a Reserve Plan which usually results from a Reserve Study.

What, actually, are some of the more typical operating costs? The biggest single category for multi-unit condos is utility costs — electric power, gas perhaps, (or oil), and water. Staffing costs can be high as well ... a building superintendent, a property manager, a front-desk security person. Calling in repair people for minor repairs, contracting out the landscaping and snow removal work are other on-going costs. The biggest category for townhouse developments or single-family homes would be costs related to grounds maintenance.

One of the principal characteristics of these operating costs is their predictability. They are, simply, very predictable. For one thing, the forecasting horizon is short. One year in most cases. For example, thinking of weather forecasts, that the weatherman's outlook for tomorrow is likely to be a lot more accurate than his outlook for next week. Operating cost predictions are similar. They're not for the distant future, they occur over the next few months, so they're not likely to be out by much.

Reserve fund expenditures have an "air" of predictability. They're derived from a "study" which has the sound of something quite profound and unassailable. And they're presented in voluminous detail which seems impressive. But reserves expenditures, in actual fact, are often astoundingly out-of-whack. It's not unusual to estimate that a boiler overhaul will cost $X only to find that when they "open her up" they find it's deteriorated so much that a new boiler's required. It's also not unusual to incur totally unexpected and very large bills for occurrences that are by their very nature unpredictable. Damage from severe weather conditions, new town by-laws that require special safety and security installations, and so on.

Reserve fund plans generally span 20 or 30 years, and even if you build in an inflation factor, it doesn't begin to insulate the plan from cost changes that bear no relationship to ordinary inflation calculations.

## Controlling Operating Costs and Reserve Fund Expenditures

Operating costs, paid out of your annual operating budget, are relatively controllable. Major repair expanses, paid out of reserves, are not. If a severe winter resulted in higher outlays for snow-removal, you might cut back on the flower beds a bit to keep the "grounds" category within budget. You can decide to give the superintendant a raise in pay, or not to. The *results* of some operating cut-backs, however, are quite visible. When housekeeping is less frequent, or if the front-desk is not occupied on weekends, people are apt to notice, and, of course, complain. But that's another story.

Reserve fund expenditures are generally intended to be made "as scheduled" in the reserves plan. But sometimes they have to be incurred earlier than the plan called for. If balcony railings have become unsafe, there's no choice but to get them fixed. So the timing can be off from the planner's estimates. Similarly, the bills you get for the work can differ, sometimes greatly, from the predicted levels. It's easy to imagine that a boiler replacement job predicted in 2011, to be carried out in 2017, might be required earlier, or come in at a price at some considerable variance from the plan numbers.

As you have seen, there are considerable differences between the behavior of operating expense items and reserve fund items. But in summary, what it boils down to is … there is NO causal relationship between operating costs and reserve expenditures. Tackle your planning for these two kinds of costs as two distinctly separate exercises. Your plans and budgets will be much better if you do.

# Your Reserve Fund Components List

## The Most Comprehensive List Available
If you already have a reserve fund plan, here's a good chance to check and make sure you're not overlooking anything. If you're creating a plan this list will get you off to a fast start.

---

The basic building blocks of a reserve fund study are the physical elements for which repair and replacement work is anticipated. The estimated costs of the work form an integral part of the plan, and estimates for the timing of the repairs and replacements are critical to arrive at annual estimates of the total costs.

It's generally agreed that the costs related to reserve funds are ...

    (1) ... connected with work on components that are part of the "common" property. That is, these are not costs that are normally borne by the individual co-owners for maintenance of their own units.

    (2) ... usually built and maintained to take care of major expenditures. Smaller day-to-day fix-ups come out of the operating budget. Often, properties set a figure, say, $1000 and over, for work that is eligible for funding from the reserve balances.

The list we have compiled is intended to serve two purposes. One is to help those who are in the early stages of creating a reserve fund plan. A not surprising question is, "Where do we start?" Our list is a good starting place.

Our second goal is to have the list serve as a checklist for those who regularly carry out inspections or for those who engage professionals to do it. It may seem bizarre to our readers, but your authors have seen instances where components that are obvious repair- or replacement-candidates have been overlooked by plan preparers. When that happens, the component needs work performed on it, but no money for the work has been set aside!

One additional point. The list is as reasonably comprehensive as we've been able to make it. We say "reasonably" because there's bound to be a property out there that has a water-slide, or a woodworking room that we haven't listed here. We think for 99% of our readers, our components list will serve you well.

**Copies of this Components List are available**
**free of charge,**
**as a WORD file.**

To order your Components List go to
oliver-group.com/rfund
and click on "More Free Things".

With the file you can install the list on your computer and this will enable you to print it out, to edit it, to copy it into an Excel file, and so on.

## SITE WORKS
### HARD LANDSCAPING
Curbs
Patios
Pedestrian Walks - Interlock/Concrete
Pedestrian Walks - Asphalt
Pedestrian Walks - Other
Fencing - Wood
Fencing - Chain Link
Fencing - Metal
Fencing - (Decorative) Masonry
Roadways / Driveways (Asphalt)
Roadways / Driveways (Repair/overlay)
Roadways / Driveways (Painting)
Garbage/Loading Pad
Planter - Concrete/Stone
Planter - Timber
Stairs - Concrete
Stairs - Wood
Flag Pole
Site / Street Furnishings
Wood Deck
Signs
Painting
Other
### SOFT LANDSCAPING
Trees
Other
### AMENITIES (excludes Recreation Centres)
Tennis Courts
Tennis Court Fence
Playground Structures
Pools - Shell Repair/Replacement
Pools - Pavement/Deck
Gazebos
Utility Sheds
Mechanical/Utility Building
Other
## STRUCTCTURE
### BUILDING
Foundations
Foundation Wall Damp Proofing
Sub-Structures
Superstructures
Stairs
Other
### SITE
Stairs (Concrete)
Stairs (Wood)

Handrails & Guards
Retaining Walls
Decks/Docks
Other
### SLAB/DECKS (Balcony)
Structural Systems (Conc. Repair)
Guards/Railings/Dividers (Concrete)
Guards/Railings/Dividers (Other)
Guards/Railings/Dividers (Painting)
Waterproofing Systems
Sealer
Other (Minor Repair)
### PARKING GARAGES
Structural Systems - Minor Repair
Structural Systems - Major Repair
Structural Systems - Roof Slab Repair
Intermediate Slab Waterproofing Sys (Thin System - Ureteoprene)
Intermediate Slab Waterproofing Systems (Thick System - asp
Roof Slab Waterproofing Systems (Under Paved Areas) + Over
Roof Slab Waterproofing Systems (Under Landscaping) + Over
Roof Slab Waterproofing Systems (Excluding Overburden)
Ramps - Structural
Ramps - Asphalt Topping/Waterproofing
Ramps - Retaining Wall
Drains - Ramp Trench and Others
Wall Waterproofing
Slab-on-Grade Sealer
Slab-on-Grade Repair
Roof Expansion Joints
Painting
Ceiling Finish - Tile
Other

## BUILDING ENVELOPE
### WALLS
Masonry (Brick Veneer)
Concrete (Precast Panels)
Concrete (CIPC)
EIFS
Steel Siding
Curtain Wall

Metal Panel
Stucco
General Repairs
Other (i.e. flashing, stone work)
**COATINGS**
Concrete
Aluminum (Windows/Panels)
General (Doors, Windows, Fence)
**DOORS**
Glazed Entrance Door System
Service Doors
Balcony / Patio Doors
Overhead Doors
Overhead Doors - Mechanical
Hardware
Other
**WINDOWS**
Windows
Glazing (IG Unit Replacement)
Weather-stripping
Cap Beading
Other
**SEALANTS**
Cladding Joints - Face Seal (1
Stage)
Cladding Joints - 2 Stage
Windows and Doors
Sealant Repair Allowance
**ROOFING / TERRACES**
Sloped Roofing - Metal
Sloped Roofing - Other
Flat Roof - REPAIR
Flat (Conventional) - Mod Bit
Flat (Conventional) - BUR
Flat (Conventional) - Single-Ply
Flat (Inverted) - Mod Bit
Flat (Inverted) - BUR
Flat (Inverted) - Single-Ply
Flat Roofing - EPDM
Flat Roofing - PVC
Terrace (Waterproofing and
Overburden)
Flashings (Base and Cap - Metal)
Hatches
Skylights
Eaves troughs & Downspouts
Soffit and Fascia
Parapets (Concrete)
Wood Deck / Catwalk
Safety Anchors
Canopy (Canvas)
Other

**MECHANICAL SYSTEMS**

**SITE SYSTEMS**
Irrigation
Domestic Water Main
Buried Services (Repair Contin-
gency)
Other
**DRAINAGE SYSTEMS**
Sanitary Drainage System
Storm Drainage System
Pumps (Sump)
Roof Drains
**DOMESTIC WATER SYSTEMS**
Boilers (Overhaul)
Boilers (Replace)
Hot Water Storage Tanks (Re-
Lining)
Hot Water Storage Tanks (Re-
place)
Circulating & Booster Pumps
Domestic Water System (Type M)
- COLD
Domestic Water System (Type M)
- HOT
Domestic Water System (Type L)
- COLD
Domestic Water System (Type L)
- HOT
Domestic Water System (Galva-
nized)
Domestic Hot Water Recirculation
System (+5yrs for Type L)
Domestic Hot Water Booster
Pump
Domestic Hot Water Circulation
Pumps
Domestic Hot Water Heat Ex-
changer
Water Softeners
Insulation
Valves
**HEATING SYSTEMS**
Boilers (Overhaul)
Boilers (Replace)
Circulating Pumps
Unit Heaters (Fan Coil - Hydronic)
Unit Heaters (Fan Coil - Electric)
Risers/Piping
Valves
Insulation
Auxiliary Hydronic Heating Sys-
tems
Chemical Treatment
Garage Heating
Other

131

## COOLING SYSTEMS
Chiller (Centrifugal)
Chiller (Reciprocating)
Cooling Tower
Condenser Water Pump
Circulating Pumps
Fan Coil Units
Heat Pump Units
Thru-Wall Units
Distribution Systems
Window Units
Split System AC
Air-Cooled Condensers
Other

## VENTILATION SYSTEMS
Make-Up Air Systems (Overhaul)
Make-Up Air Systems (Replace)
Central Exhaust Fans
Parking Garage Exhaust Fans
CO Detection Systems
Pressurization Fans & Fire Alarm
Interlock
Unit Exhaust Fans
Humidification / Dehumidification
Systems
Ducting
Diffusers & Grilles
Controls
Other

## WASTE DISPOSAL SYSTEMS
Garbage Compactor
Garbage Chute
Garbage Chute Doors
Other

## SWIMMING/WHIRLPOOL EQUIPMENT
Sand Filters/ Filtration System
Circulation Pumps
Chlorinator / Brominator
Electric Booster Pumps
Boilers (Overhaul)
Boilers (Replace)
Heat Exchangers
Dehumidification Systems
Shell Repair
Other

## OTHER EQUIPMENT
Sauna
Common Area Plumbing Fixtures
Janitor's Closet (Plumbing Fixtures)
Other

# ELECTRICAL SYSTEMS
## ELECTRICAL SUPPLY and DISTRIBUTION
Power Supply (Transformer)
Power Distribution
Panel boards and Sub-Circuits
Main Panel/Switch Gear
Intermediate Panel
Suite Panel
Other

## LIGHTING SYSTEMS
Corridors (Fluorescent)
Building Common Areas
Building Service Areas
Building Service Areas (Stairwells)
Garage Lighting
Exterior Lighting (HID/HPS)
Exterior Lighting (Incandescent)
Other

## HEATERS
Baseboard
Fan Heaters
Miscellaneous Heating Equipment

## AUXILIARY SYSTEMS
Pipe Heat Tracing
Exterior Snow & Ice Melt Systems (Electric)
Exterior Snow & Ice Melt Systems (Glycol)
Security Systems (Intercom)
Security Systems (Enterphone)
Security Systems (Access Card System)
Security Systems (CCTV)
Security Systems (Suite Security - VIC)
Other

# LIFE SAFETY SYSTEMS
## FIRE DETECTION
Fire Alarm Panel
Annunciator
Detection Devices
Signal Devices
Other

## SPRINKLER SYSTEMS
Standpipe and Siamese Connection
Fire Pump
Jockey Pump

Fire Hose Cabinets (Hose)
Distribution (Piping, Valves and Heads)
Valves
Sprinkler Heads
Pipes
**EMERGENCY SYSTEMS**
Generator - Overhaul
Emergency Power Supply (Diesel)
Emergency Power Supply (Battery)
Emergency Power Supply (Gas)
Emergency Lighting Systems
Exit Lighting Fixtures
Transfer Switch
Panic Hardware
Panic Hardware

## ELEVATOR
**Cab Refurbishment**
Panic Hardware
Panic Hardware
Panic Hardware
Panic Hardware
**Control Modernization**
**Equipment Upgrades/Replacements**
Hoisting Equipment
Motor
Cab Structure
Infrared/Door Operators/Protection
Barrier-Free Upgrades
Code Changes & Vandalism
Machine Room Cooling
Other
**Other Conveyance Equipment**

## INTERIOR FINISHES / FURNISHINGS
**CORRIDORS**
Flooring (carpet)
Flooring (Tile)
Wall Finish (Paint)
Wall Finish (Papered)
Ceiling Finish
Trim / Accessories
**LOBBY/LOUNGE**
Flooring (Granite/Marble)
Flooring (Ceramic Tile)

Flooring (Carpet)
Wall Finish

Ceiling Finish
Furniture
Elevator Lobbies
Other
**RECREATION AREAS**
General Rec Centre Finishes (All Finishes)
General Rec Centre Finishes (All Finishes)
General Rec Centre Finishes (All Finishes)
Swimming Pool (Paint Tank and Deck)
Swimming Pool (Paint Tank and Deck)
Sauna
Whirlpool
Showers/Change Room Finishes
Change Rooms (Lockers)
Exercise Room (Finishes)
Exercise Room (Equipment)
Games/Hobby Room
Squash/Racquetball Court
Party Room/ Lounge / Kitchen
Craft Room / Other Rooms
Equipment and Furnishings
Other
**SERVICE AREAS**
Management Office
Board Room
Laundry Room (Fixture/Appliances)
Laundry Room (Finishes)
Stairwells - Handrails
Stairwells - Floor/Tread Finish
Stairwells - Paint
Garbage Disposal (Finishes)
Locker Rooms
M & E Service Rooms
Guest/Super Suite - Refurbish
Washrooms
Misc Interior Finishes & Equipment
**INTERIOR WINDOWS & DOORS**
Suite Doors (ULC Rated)
Vestibule Door Systems
Service Room, Common Rooms, and Access to Exit Doors (Metal
Other Interior Doors
Interior Glazing

Door Hardware
**OTHER - Unit Interior**
Demising Walls
Interior Doors (Hollow)
Flooring - Carpet
Flooring - Wood
Flooring - Ceramic Tile
Flooring - Vinyl
Walls - Paint
Walls - Other
Cabinetry
Fridge
Stove
Toilets
Bathroom Fixtures
Kitchen Sink & Fixtures

# HELPFUL
# LINKS

Many readers of "Essentials" will already be familiar with links to websites that relate to co-owned properties. But the make-up of the market is constantly changing — board members in particular are likely to be newcomers to the topic of reserve funds.

This chapter is not intended to be a definitive collection of all possible links. Just the opposite, actually. We're simply listing a few that you may want to explore. The first two of them actually provide links, themselves, to a great number of additional sites.

### Community Associations Institute
cai.online.org
A large U.S.-based organization offering a wide variety of information and resources.

### Canadian Condominium Institute
cci.ca, for CCI National. ccitoronto.org, for CCI Toronto
Description similar to CAI above.

### ECHO — The Executive Council of Homeowners
echo-ca.org
ECHO is a nonprofit membership corporation dedicated to assisting California homeowners associations. This organization's website posts articles and information that is of interest to all homeowner communities.

### ACMO
### Association of Condominium Managers of Ontario
acmo.org
An Ontario-based organization for property managers and other professionals

## Community Associations Network
communityassociations.net/index.html
In their own words — a resource center for those who live in, govern or work with condominium, homeowner and property owner associations. CAN links to articles and information around the Internet. By clicking Subscribe to Newsletter you will receive a bi-monthly CAN ... Community Associations newsletter

## Association Times
associationtimes.com/index.htm
A resource for disseminating timely information to property owners' associations.

## Regenesis.net
regenesis.net/
Provides innovative management strategies for boards, managers and developers. "Makes HOA living the carefree experience it is intended to be".

## HOATalk
hoatalk.com/
HOATalk is a members-only discussion forum where thousands of HOA Leaders meet to share ideas and learn.

## The State of California
The California Department of Real Estate offers, on its website, three useful manuals of interest to Boards and professional service providers. The booklets are ... Reserve Study Guidelines for Homeowners Association Budgets ... Operating Cost Manual for Homeowners Associations (includes "useful life" estimates) ... and ... Association Budget Worksheet[1].

## RFund
oliver-group.com/rfund
Our own website. Besides its focus on RFund software, the site includes some useful free giveaways, as well as a Viewpoints section.

---

[1] The links are very long and do not lend themselves to copying out. We will be pleased to send them to you by e-mail so that you can simply "click" to reach each particular booklet. Contact us a rfund@oliver-group.com

# RFund Software
# A Perfect Fit

### This Book, and RFund.
### They Go Together Like a Horse and Carriage

Our book is founded on the principles associated with the main-tenance of adequate reserve fund balances. The underlying principles are translated into practical methods for arriving at healthy reserves and keeping them that way. These very same methods are embodied in RFund. It's the product of Oliver Interactive, Inc. that's operated by one of this book's co-authors. This chapter provides the opportunity to explore what RFund is able to do for you, as a board member, a reserves planner or a property manager.

---

### RFund's Job

Its main job is to take raw inputs and translate them into workable plans. The principal inputs are the estimates of your property's components in respect to their remaining useful life and the costs of periodically replacing or repairing them. Using this data along with a rate for predicted inflation and earned interest, RFund allows the user to set owners'' contributions levels that will result in comfortable future fund balances.

### Adequacy Ratios

A click of your mouse provides proven yardsticks to measure the Adequacy of your reserve balances. It's great for all the alternative funding options you'd like to try. Less guesswork, better reserve plans!

### Smooth Plans are Better

Plans with a minimum of jagged peaks and hollows are easier to fund which means they're more acceptable to unit owners. RFund's Condition and Funding Indexes help you arrive at optimal expenditure and contributions patterns.

### Quick What-Ifs

Trying out alternate funding schedules is a snap. You'll see the effects graphically and in numbers, instantly.

### Escalations

Try funding escalation factors across any time-span in the plan period. Fine-tune the funding schedule for optimal acceptance

## Plan Freshening

Keep your reserve plan updated regularly. Plug in actual expenditure dollars to replace planned amounts as they come in. (Quarterly is good!).

## Components Inputs

Track actual expenditures as they occur. Update all your components expenditures estimates right in RFund remarkable "Treeview" grid!

## Easy-Share Process

RFund's copyrighted display can easily be shared with others. Send copies to your fellow Board Members, and, when asked, to real estate people and prospective buyers.

## Special Prices for Planners and Property Managers

For service providers we have a steeply declining price schedule. So you can use one RFund installation very affordably, for all your properties.

## Free Quick-Start Offer

We'll do the data input for a couple of your real plans, to get you started. In fact, we'll even do it for the Free 60-Day Trial copy that you can download. Trying is believing!

## Plan Creation, for Planners

RFund uses the Cash Flow approach to reserve plan creation. Simpler and faster to do and every bit as solid as the full-funding system. Easier for clients to understand too!

## Great Standard Features

A far cry from "standard". And they're found nowhere else. "Useful as all get-out". **Property Facts** with loads of info at your fingertips, the **Investment Log** to stay on top of your reserves money, the **per-unit and per-month** outputs, **Everyday Notes** to assemble all the little things in a hurry. **Funding Indexes** to keep your contributions smooth. There's just no end to it!

## Free for Two Months

You get the 100% real thing to use for 60 days. To continue with RFund simply pay to re-activate your program.

## One-time Installation

RFund's Perpetual License plan means you download RFund once and it's good forever. (You can opt, instead, for a low-cost yearly-renewable license).

For Additional Information
or to order, go to
oliver-group.com/rfund

Made in the USA
Charleston, SC
14 May 2011